THE CHURCH'S USE OF THE BIBLE

Past and Present

THE
CHURCH'S USE OF
THE BIBLE

Past and Present

Edited by D. E. Nineham

LONDON
S·P·C·K
1963

First published in 1963 by
S.P.C.K.
Holy Trinity Church
Marylebone Road
London N.W.1

Printed in Great Britain by
Billing and Sons, Guildford

© The Trustees of the Society for
Promoting Christian Knowledge, 1963

Contents

CONTENTS

Preface

PERHAPS the best way of making clear the purpose and scope of the following lectures will be to reproduce in substance the brief statement with which the first of them was introduced on 1 March 1960:

The year 1957 was of great importance for the study of theology in London University. The University authorities decided to strengthen the Faculty by inaugurating two new chairs and a readership in theological subjects with a further chair to follow at the end of the quinquennium. As one of the newly appointed professors I asked myself what I could do to contribute to the marking of the occasion and decided to arrange a series of public lectures related to my chair of Divinity. It seemed right that it should be on a subject of interest and concern to contemporary theologians, and also a subject whose ventilation would be of value to the life of the contemporary Church. I could think of nothing more important in both these respects than the question of the principles of interpretation which must be applied to the Bible in order to make it yield its message in a form intelligible and significant for our time. This subject has, it is true, been very widely discussed of recent years, but comparatively little attempt has been made, so far as I know, to discover how our predecessors in the long course of Christian theology have dealt with the matter. There is, of course, the very useful volume of Alleyn Lectures edited by my colleague, Professor C. W. Dugmore, some fifteen years ago,[1] but in view of all the thought that has been given to the question of biblical interpretation in the intervening period, it seemed that the time might be ripe for a rather fuller treatment of the subject from the historical point of view, and that such a treatment might well have several morals for us. And so I ventured to ask a number of extremely eminent specialists in various periods of Christian history if they would each give a lecture for us on the way in which the theologians of their par-

[1] *The Interpretation of the Bible*, S.P.C.K., 1944.

ticular period approached this matter. We should be very honoured that every one of these scholars readily agreed to come, so that what we hear about each of the periods in the past will come with the authority of an acknowledged expert. I am sure that you will be as grateful to them all as I am myself.

In the event, two of those who had agreed to contribute to the series died before they could do so. When Bishop Rawlinson died in July 1960 Professor Lampe very kindly agreed to give the seventh lecture in his place. Meanwhile, owing to the illness of Dr Norman Sykes, who was to have given the sixth lecture, the last three lectures in the series had been postponed, in the hope that Dr Sykes might be able to give his lecture later. After his death it was too late to ask any other scholar to prepare a lecture in his place, but Dr Edward Carpenter has very kindly agreed to supply a paper on the Bible in the eighteenth century for the printed version of the lectures.

Since I personally am deeply indebted to Norman Sykes perhaps I may reproduce here some part of the tribute to him with which I prefaced the last lecture in the series, given two months after his death.

I cannot begin the concluding lecture in this series, to which he was to have contributed, without paying some tribute to the memory of Dr Sykes. It was in this College that he began the career of teaching and research which was to be so exceptionally and deservedly distinguished; such was his distinction that it can be said without risk of affront to any scholar who may undertake to supply a lecture on the eighteenth century when this series is published, that the series can never be quite the same without a contribution from Norman Sykes. For there was about him, both as a man and a scholar, something unique, a certain combination of learning, robust common sense, and sheer humanity, which those who were familiar with it will never cease to savour with gratitude and affection. . . . Here was a highly entertaining personality, a fine scholar, a good Christian, and I think we may say a genuinely great man, who will be deeply missed by the Churches, the Universities, and his many friends.

It remains to thank the authorities of University of London King's College, by whose generosity these lectures were made possible and also my former secretary, Mrs. A. R. Wilkinson, and her successor Miss D. E. Williams, for the very great contribution they have made to the organizing of the lectures and the production of this book.

D. E. Nineham

The Bible in the New Testament Period

C. K. BARRETT

THERE is at least one respect in which the present lecture must differ from every other in the series of which it is the first. In every other lecture it will be possible to look back upon the Bible as a whole, and to study it as it appeared to a group or generation of Christians. It may prove that some were more interested in the Old Testament, others in the New; but all were aware of both Testaments, and when they read the one they were affected in their understanding of it, if only unconsciously, by their knowledge of the other.

To-day, however, we are taken by our subject into a period in which, by definition, the whole Bible had not come into being. In the "New Testament period" the Old Testament existed, but the New Testament was only in process of becoming; we can no longer view the Bible from without, but actually stand within it. In fact, we are in a position to make the best of two worlds. If we went back to the Old Testament period, we should find ourselves with no Bible in the proper sense at all, but only a book in process of development, not yet capable of exerting influence upon anything extraneous to itself. In the later ages, the Bible is a closed and complete unity, exerting influence as a finished body of authoritative literature. But in the New Testament period we can on the one hand trace the origin of the New Testament books in the unwritten traditions that preceded them, and on the other observe the influence of the already complete Old Testament. Indeed, we may and must unite these two themes and study the way in which the Old Testament affected the development of the New Testament tradition and literature.

I

This course of lectures as a whole presupposes the belief, in which all Christians are agreed, that in age after age the Bible has exerted a creative influence upon the lives of men and women, and upon the life of the Church, releasing from itself fresh supplies of energy and understanding, like a volcano erupting from time to time, and hurling forth its fiery streams. To-day we have the opportunity of studying the geological processes through which the volcano came into existence. We may hope to give some account of the rock formations which have determined the shape of what we see before us, and also to learn something about the way in which the external shape is related to the invisible source of heat and energy. I mean by this that our study of the influence of the finished Old Testament tradition upon the developing New Testament tradition may help to explain the form of the latter, and that relation of both to God and his acts in which their authority and vitality consist.

It was not in Christian circles only that the Old Testament exerted a formative and creative influence in the New Testament period. At first, the Church formed only one among a number of groups within Judaism, all of which looked upon what we call the Old Testament as their sacred and authoritative literature. All were consciously dependent upon it, and all essayed the task of interpreting it in the light of their own convictions and circumstances. A full discussion of the Bible in the New Testament period would involve an account of all these interpretations as well as the Christian interpretation, and though time does not permit so wide a survey our discussion of the origins of the New Testament in the light of the influence upon it of the Old Testament would be much impoverished if we did not briefly consider them.

Perhaps the simplest field, and the best in which to begin, is that of Alexandrian Judaism. Not that there is no subtlety and profundity in, for example, Philo's use of the Old Testament; on the contrary. But the motive with which Philo works, and his method, are both of them relatively clear.[1] A man, nearly the whole of whose literary output is devoted to the exposition of the Bible, may be safely supposed to be primarily concerned with the meaning and impact of Scripture. He may be a bad, a misleading exegete; this makes no difference. Philo's intention was to commend what he conceived to be the biblical faith of his own people, and his method was the exposition of the source of this faith, Scripture itself.

This intention and this method were almost inevitable in one nurtured in Alexandrian Judaism. It is impossible to deny that the Jewish community in Alexandria was exposed to powerful influences from the Hellenistic world, but this truth has sometimes been over-emphasized at the expense of another, equally important—the truth that Alexandrian Jews were as acutely conscious of the Bible as any of their compatriots. The memorial of this truth is the Septuagint, the first great biblical translation, consistently glorified by Alexandrian tradition.[2]

Philo himself was a loyal Jew. It is unnecessary to prove this from his writings; it is superabundantly demonstrated by his willingness, on behalf of his fellow-Jews, to put his head inside the lion's mouth by leading a deputation to the emperor Gaius.[3] Readiness for martyrdom is no proof of orthodoxy, but it is a good enough sign of loyalty and sincerity. As a good Jew, Philo was horrified by pagan religions, and desired to propagate his own faith. In setting it forth he adhered resolutely to the biblical pattern, and expounded large parts of the Pentateuch verse by verse.

Philo thus presents himself to us as a Jew, and as a student

---

[1] Though it cannot be claimed that they are undisputed. It must suffice here to recall such names as E. Bréhier, E. R. Goodenough, H. A. A. Kennedy, J. Klausner, W. L. Knox, E. Schürer, H. Windisch, H. Wolfson.

[2] See the legendary account of the origin of the translation in the Epistle of Aristeas. If this document was intended to support one form of LXX text against others, this serves only to emphasize the important place accorded by the local Jews to their Bible. Philo himself bears witness to an annual festival held in his day with great enthusiasm "to pay reverence to the spot on which the translation first shed its light, and to render God thanks for a benefit, ancient yet ever new" (de Vit. Mos. ii. 41).

[3] See his In Flaccum and Legatio ad Gaium.

and expositor of the Old Testament. It would be idle to deny that he was at the same time a citizen of the Hellenistic world, thoroughly familiar with both the substance and the form of its thought. It is well known that he succeeded in finding in the Old Testament Platonism, Stoicism, and Neo-Pythagoreanism for which Moses and the prophets were certainly not responsible. He achieved this result by the method of allegory, of which his use seems at times to be quite irresponsible: he reads out of his text thoughts which he has first implanted in it. His motive, however, was never conscious falsification, but that of the missionary. Convinced that Judaism was the true and final religion, and convinced too that there was much truth in what he had read of Greek philosophy, it was inevitable that he should commend his religion by demonstrating, by means which satisfied his conscience and intelligence—whether or not they satisfy ours—that it had anticipated and excelled all other founts of wisdom.

Philo's task was the reinterpretation of the Old Testament in the light of the Hellenic milieu in which he lived, and for this reason he will always be important to students of the New Testament, for the New Testament writers also were engaged in the task of commending the Old Testament faith to the Greek world. But more important for our present purpose is the observation that, though Philo on the one hand, and, on the other, Paul, John, and the other New Testament writers, were all of them reinterpreting the Old Testament, he produced nothing like a *New* Testament, which could stand on at least equal terms with the Old, whereas they did so. The reason is clear. Philo can only depotentiate the Old Testament; he can remove difficulties (such as apparent anthropomorphisms), and bring to light hidden truth and hidden beauty; but he cannot recapture the creative life which made the Law and the Prophets. He can at best pass on the Old Testament second-hand; more polished, perhaps, but less virile and energetic. He lacks the dynamic of a new divine act, such as the New Testament writers believed they had witnessed.

4

Philo may be dismissed (though wrongfully) as more a Hellenist than a biblicist; the Rabbis at all events will not be disposed of in this way. Mishnah, Talmud, and Midrashim are all steeped in the Old Testament, and could not exist without it. It is true that in them also we meet exegesis which has little to do with its text, but the honest intention of the Rabbis to determine not only their writings but their lives by the Old Testament is beyond dispute.

The traditional teaching by means of which Judaism preserved, developed, and handed on the religion of the Old Testament may be divided into two parts. The *halakah* represented the detailed application of the Old Testament law to the changing circumstances in which the readers of the Old Testament lived. These circumstances were partly external, and the Old Testament law inevitably became far more complex as precepts and institutions which originated in a relatively simple and undeveloped rural society were perpetuated in an urban society where life and its relationships were more advanced and complicated. The changing circumstances were also inward, in that men came to look upon many matters in a new light; for example, the *lex talionis* was progressively modified, till instead of requiring "an eye for an eye and a tooth for a tooth" men were content with a monetary compensation. In innumerable *halakoth* the Rabbis carried through this progressive application and adaptation of the written Law.

The second line of development was that of *haggadah*, a word which defies precise definition. It is not the product of technical legal exegesis, but is essentially popular—popular narrative, popular preaching. The old biblical stories are told and retold, and embroidered in the telling; new stories, some true, some legendary, some partly true and partly legendary, are added to them. The whole is used to point morals—religious, ethical, and sometimes political and nationalistic.

That the Rabbis were by no means out of touch with the

Greek world is to-day more and more recognized;[1] but beyond question the total effect of this halakic and haggadic tradition is to create what may almost be described as an imaginary world in which the Old Testament lives on, a world continuous with the Old Testament.

There is close formal resemblance between the Rabbinic use of the Old Testament and that which we find in the New Testament. There are common citation formulas,[2] common exegetical methods,[3] and common exegetical results.[4] These resemblances lie upon the surface, and any competent observer can detect them. It is equally easy to detect the fundamental difference between the Rabbis and the apostles in the conviction of the latter that the Messiah had come in the person of Jesus of Nazareth. But it is our object to dig deeper if we can, and to see the difference between the kind of literature which the Rabbinic movement produced, and that which was created in Christian circles.

On the Rabbinic side, the new material which accompanied and interpreted the Old Testament, that is, the *halakah* and *haggadah*, took the form of a tradition[5] which, it was claimed, went back to Moses himself. The classical statement about the tradition is in Aboth 1. 1: Moses received the Law from Sinai and committed it to Joshua, and Joshua to the elders, and the elders to the Prophets; and the Prophets committed it to the men of the Great Synagogue. By "the Law" is meant here the Oral Law—the tradition. Moses received two laws on Mount Sinai, the written and the oral. The latter had through a thousand years or more persisted alongside the former; having

---

[1] See for example W. L. Knox, *St Paul and the Church of Jerusalem*, 1939, pp. 54, 91, 100, 113.

[2] The καθὼς γέγραπται and καθὼς εἴρηται of the New Testament are easy to parallel.

[3] See for example Paul's use of the *gezerah shawah* in Rom. 4, to which J. Jeremias draws attention in *Studia Paulina* (edited by J. N. Sevenster and W. C. van Unnik, 1953), pp. 149ff.

[4] See for example John 1. 51; 8. 56.

[5] The New Testament itself uses the word παράδοσις; e.g. Mark 7. 3, 5, 8, 9, 13.

the same origin it had equal authority. This is not a belief that the historian can share; but it is important to understand its significance. The Old Testament itself was authoritative, but its authority lay in its origin, rather than in any immediate applicability to the present time. Venerated, loved, and obeyed, it was nevertheless out of touch, and could become effective only through an interpreting tradition. But this tradition could be used for this purpose only if it too were authoritative; and the only way in which the Rabbis could give it authority was to trace it back to the same origin as the written law which it expounded and applied. The one source of truth and authority was Mount Sinai.

We shall see later that the contents of the New Testament also may be described in terms of tradition, a tradition which brings the hidden truth of the Old Testament to light and applies it to the present. The significant difference however lies in the fact that the New Testament tradition not only illuminates the present by means of the Old Testament but also takes its origin in the present. Mount Sinai is not the only creative moment in history. "I received", says Paul, "of the Lord" (1 Cor. 11. 23). The Rabbis could speak of the withdrawal of the Holy Spirit and the cessation of prophecy; not so the apostles. Over against that which was said to them of old time there now rings out a new "But I say unto you"—not indeed destroying, but fulfilling the old. The New Testament tradition is not a mere shadow of the written tradition of the Old Testament, but a new creation.

For a third example of the use, and the effect, of the Old Testament within non-Christian Judaism we may turn to Qumran and the so-called Dead Sea Scrolls. Where much is questionable, there can be no question that the Qumran community founded itself upon the scriptures. Among the documents recovered from the caves, manuscripts of the Old Testament have a prominent place. Doubtless they were essential to the community's life. Along with the Old Testament manuscripts, there is liturgical material (whose model is undoubtedly the Old Testament Psalter); apocalyptic material; legislation (that is, a special *halakah*, based like that of the Rabbis upon the Old Testament law); and exegesis, of which the best-known example is the Habakkuk commentary.

It is natural to compare the Qumran exegesis with that of Philo. Both proceed with evident veneration for the text of the Old Testament, but their methods and results differ widely. It is characteristic of Philo to generalize upon what he reads. A particular historical statement becomes the starting-point for moral and analogical deductions of universal application. Thus Abraham's reception of the three strangers [1] leads Philo to praise the virtue of hospitality, and then to show that hospitality is but the by-product of a greater virtue, piety. Leaving the literal exposition (τὰ τῆς ῥητῆς ἀποδόσεως) he goes on to allegorize the Three, and to see in them God in his unique self-existence, flanked by his accompanying Powers, the ruling and the creative, by means of which he is known. And so on— for Philo has yet more to say.

The commentary, or *pesher*, on Habakkuk works in the opposite direction. Moving away from the more general it works towards the more particular, and finds fulfilment of the words of Habakkuk in recent events. For example, the interpretation of Hab. 2. 4, 5, 6 is as follows:[2]

> *But the righteous shall live by his faith.* This means all the doers of the law in the house of Judah, whom God will rescue from the house of judgement because of their labour and their faith in the teacher of righteousness. *Moreover, wealth is treacherous, an arrogant man, and will not abide. His greed is as wide as Sheol; and he like death has never enough. To him are gathered all the nations, and to him are assembled all the peoples. Shall not all of them take up their taunt against him, in scoffing derision of him, and say, "Woe to him who heaps up, but it is not his own! How long will he load himself with pledges?"?* This means the wicked priest, who was named according to the truth when he first took office; but when he had begun to rule in Israel, his heart was lifted up, and he forsook God and

---

[1] *De Abrahamo* 107–32, using Gen. 18.
[2] The translation is from Millar Burrows, *The Dead Sea Scrolls*, 1956, p. 368.

betrayed the statutes because of wealth. He plundered and assembled the wealth of men of violence who rebelled against God. He took the wealth of peoples, adding to himself iniquity and guilt: and ways of abomination he wrought, in all impurity of uncleanness.

In the Qumran manuscript, but not in Philo, the significance of the Old Testament words is found in their fulfilment in recent events. This means that, in its exegesis, the Qumran manuscript stands much nearer to the New Testament than does Philo, for the New Testament writers also believed that they were witnessing the fulfilment of the Old Testament, and the process of creative fulfilment is that which generates the New Testament out of the Old. It thus becomes necessary to compare the two notions of fulfilment, that of the New Testament and that of Qumran. The two circles share the belief that in their time certain prophecies have been fulfilled; that is, certain events which the prophets predicted in more or less veiled language have now happened. The fulfilments, however, found by the Qumran writer, notwithstanding the significance of such persons as the Teacher of Righteousness, lack a focal point which could give them unity and coherence. This focal point is still to come; the major conflict between "the sons of light and the sons of darkness" is still, at the time of writing, in the future. The New Testament also looks to the future for a complete fulfilment of what the prophets foretold; but the whole process of fulfilment is focused upon a single person already known to history, Jesus Christ. That which has been fulfilled has been fulfilled in him (or at least in relation to him); that which is yet to be fulfilled will be fulfilled in him (or at least in relation to him). Moreover, in his life, death, and resurrection, an event so decisive has already taken place that the remainder of history can be regarded as its working out.[1]

We have now considered three sectors of Judaism, in each of which the Old Testament played a central and formative

[1] It is a significant fact that the New Testament contains no commentary on an Old Testament book.

9

part. Each of them presents parallels in this respect with the New Testament, but none of the parallels is complete. In Philo and Alexandrian Judaism we were able to see a missionary effort to commend to the non-Jewish world a Jewish faith rooted in the Old Testament, and at the same time a re-interpretation of the Old Testament in the light of fresh patterns of thought and experience. What was wanting was a positive and creative drive to give unity and vitality to the missionary effort and the reinterpretation. For the interpreta-tion and application of the Old Testament the Rabbis drew upon a tradition which, they believed, accompanied the Old Testament and sprang from the same source, drawing its authority not from present inspiration but from the ancient past, where alone authority resided. The New Testament writers, however, are aware of a present authority which informs their preaching and teaching. The Qumran writers are in some ways nearer to the New Testament than either Philo or the Rabbis, but here too we were able to detect differences. Where the Qumran writers are still on edge with expectation and hope, the New Testament writers are able to look back on what God has already done in decisive fulfilment of his promises.

Both the resemblances and the differences we have observed make it necessary for us to ask, What was the relation of the New Testament to the Old Testament? and, How did the Old Testament contribute to the origin of the New? We are not inquiring into the origin of the New Testament books in general terms; we are concerned with the special rôle of the Old Testament in their formation. We are not simply collecting and analysing the Old Testament quotations that occur in the New Testament, and reconstructing what has been called the "Bible of the early Church";[1] we are concerned with the creative interplay of prophet and apostle which engendered a new body of literature that could take its place alongside the

---

[1] This expression is taken from C. H. Dodd's *According to the Scriptures*, 1952, the outstanding book on the use of the Old Testament in the New.

old, not merely as equally sacred and authoritative, but as equally potent and life-giving.

It is the ultimate task of the student of the New Testament to penetrate through the literary forms of his textbook to the divine event which produced them; to hear through the words of men the Word of God; to examine (if I may return to the metaphor I used at the beginning of this lecture) the cataclysmic upheaval that produced this erupting volcano which we call the New Testament. In this upheaval, the Old Testament undoubtedly played a part; it is for us to find out what this part was.

It was not the primary part; we must not exaggerate the importance of our subject. There are areas of the New Testament which are almost entirely devoid of reference to the Old.[1] It is true that more than direct quotation is involved; even when they do not quote, the New Testament writers often use language forged by those who translated the Old Testament into Greek. Nevertheless, the Old Testament is never the primary factor in the New, which constantly looks back to, and points towards, not the Old Testament but the figure and event of Jesus Christ. It sees the Old Testament also stretching out a pointing finger directed to the same centre; but it is the centre, Jesus Christ, crucified and risen, which alone is primary and regulative. On this point the New Testament speaks with one voice. "Jews ask for signs and Greeks seek for wisdom, but we preach Christ crucified" (1 Cor. 1. 22f). "No one has ever seen God; the only-begotten Son, who is in the Father's bosom, has made him known" (John 1. 18). "Though God spoke of old to the fathers by the prophets, in various parts and various ways, he has at the end of these days spoken to us in a Son" (Heb. 1. 1f).

How then is the witness of the Old Testament related to that of the New Testament? The metaphor of the last paragraph might suggest a pair of signposts pointing to the same village,

[1] The Epistles of John, for example, contain only one direct allusion to the Old Testament.

one from the north, the other from the south; and there would be truth in this picture, for the Old Testament does point out of the past to a future event, and the New Testament looks back upon the same event as itself in the past. But the Old Testament and the New Testament are more closely related than this; it would be better to leave their chronological relationship out of account and picture them as signposts standing both on the same side of the village to which they point, one nearer to the village and, as it were, taking the more distant signpost into itself. It is, however, impossible to discuss the relation of the Old Testament to the New Testament further in these general terms. Theories and metaphors are worthless without reference to fact.

The part of the New Testament that stands in the clearest relationship with the historical event of Jesus Christ is that which we call the Synoptic Gospels. The books which bear the names of Matthew, Mark, and Luke purport to tell a story of the words and deeds of Jesus. They have therefore a special significance for our purpose.

It cannot be said that they neglect the Old Testament. There are frequent allusions to Old Testament narratives and persons, and quotations from Old Testament books; even when they are not quoting, the evangelists often use the language of the Old Testament. How then did the Old Testament affect the witness of the Synoptic Gospels to Jesus?

The reader (especially if he begins with Matthew) will probably be first impressed by the use of proof-texts—short passages from the Old Testament which (the New Testament writer claims) were predictions fulfilled by things done or said by Jesus. Lengthy illustration is unnecessary; Matt. 4. 13–16 will suffice: "[Jesus] left Nazara, and went to live at Caphar-naum-on-sea, in the districts of Zabulun and Nephthalim; in order that that which was spoken through Isaiah the prophet might be fulfilled, when he said: Land of Zabulun, land of Nephthalim, the sea-district, beyond the Jordan, Galilee of the Gentiles, the people that lived in darkness have seen a great light, and on those who lived in the region and shadow of death, on them has the light risen up."

In other words, Jesus began his ministry at Capernaum because Isa. 9. 1f said that he would do so. Mark and Luke are more restrained than Matthew in their use of proof-texts, but the difference is one of degree only. There can be no doubt that such texts played an important part in Christian argument, apologetic, and narrative in both Jewish and Gentile circles.

There are few Christian circles to-day in which they carry the same weight. They appear to us artificial; either to be erroneous, or to arise out of coincidence. This impression is not altogether wrong. It was possible to create proof-text material by manipulation, either by misinterpreting a prophet's words, as when Matthew (2. 18) applies Jeremiah's picture of the weeping Rachel (Jer. 31. 15) to the massacre of the children by Herod, or by rewriting historical narrative, as when Matthew, who, alone of the Synoptists, quotes Zech. 9. 9 ("Thy king cometh unto thee . . . riding upon an ass, and upon a colt the foal of an ass"), modifies the Marcan account of the Triumphal Entry so as to portray Jesus as using two animals (21. 2, 7). Again, the modern reader cannot fail to wonder whether there is any connection beyond coincidence between Zechariah's "Smite the shepherd, and the sheep shall be scattered" (13. 7, quoted in Mark 14. 27) and the arrest of Jesus and the dispersal of his followers.

To make these criticisms, however, is not to dispose of the relation between the Old Testament and the Synoptic Gospels. The manipulation of prophecy and event to make them coincide indicates a profound conviction that prophecy and event do in principle correspond, and that each finds its full meaning in the other; and coincidence can take place on a large scale only because there exists a genuine correspondence or homogeneity between the Old Testament and the gospel history. That this homogeneity exists scarcely needs to be demonstrated. It may be seen in language, and in general outlook upon life and its meaning; above all it can be seen in the idea of God which is common to the Old Testament and the Gospels. In both he is the inescapable God whose action in the past constitutes a claim upon the present, and whose action in the future is never so remote that it too does not press upon the present.

The synoptic writers composed their works in order to demonstrate, on the basis of existing tradition, that this God who, out of past and future, was always pressing upon the present, fulfilled his purposes and summed up his work for men in Jesus Christ, who came not to destroy the law and the prophets but to fulfil them. This sentence indeed, though found in Matthew only (5. 17) and the subject of a good deal of controversy, points to the place which the Old Testament holds in the synoptic tradition. How Matthew understood it appears from the remainder of the chapter, in which various legal pronouncements of the Old Testament are met by Jesus with his ἐγὼ δὲ λέγω ("but I say . . ."); the Old Testament precepts are well, but the new are better. Indeed, they are not simply "better", but bring to light what the Old Testament really meant.

The Synoptic Gospels contain free criticism of the Old Testament and its laws, but the criticism is always uttered in the conviction that Jesus makes clearer what the Old Testament meant than the Old Testament itself could do. It is this that accounts for the manipulation of proof-texts, and for the peculiar kind of correspondence with the Old Testament which the Gospels show.

The theologians of the New Testament make the same point as the historians. Christ was the end, the τέλος, of the Old Testament, in the sense that he had fulfilled it and proved it true; he had abrogated it, not by showing it to be wrong but by incorporating in himself and bringing to perfection its truth. All that the Old Testament had pointed to, he was. "However many God's promises may be, he is Yes to them all" (2 Cor. 1. 20). The theologians express this truth in characteristic ways. For Paul, "Christ is the end of the law with a view to righteousness for everyone who believes" (Rom. 10. 4). The law pointed to righteousness, and insisted that righteousness was necessary, but could never achieve it (Gal. 2. 21). Christ denied neither that the law pointed the right way, nor that it did well to require righteousness; he simply did what the law could not do (Rom. 8. 3). In the Epistle to the Hebrews we encounter the Old Testament liturgy. The author does not question that it was God's will that the Temple cultus should exist. It kept perpetually in mind the truth that man must approach God, and that to do so he must be holy. But it also kept alive the memory of sin (10. 3), without being able to cleanse the conscience (9. 9). What the Old Testament cultus could not do, Christ did; by his self-offering we are sanctified for ever, and draw near to God with full assurance (10. 10, 19–22). The Johannine treatment of the Old Testament is more subtle and does not permit itself to be summarized so simply. Yet the picture of Abraham, who in his vision of the future rejoiced to see the day of Christ (8. 56), is characteristic, and it is to John that we owe the plain statement (5. 39f) that the Old Testament scriptures, though in themselves they cannot satisfy the seeker for life, point to Christ, who gives what they cannot offer.

Of all these theologians Paul is personally known to us as no other is. It was in Christ that he perceived the true meaning of the Old Testament, which previously he had mistaken. The renewal of his understanding of the Old Testament can be seen, for example, in Rom. 10. 5–8, where he is able to set out not only an Old Testament passage describing the righteousness of the law, but also another describing the righteousness of faith. It is when he approaches the Old Testament in Christ that Paul can see that it too bears witness to justification by faith. It is quite wrong to suggest that Paul fastened his understanding of the Old Testament upon Christ; it was Christ who gave him a new understanding of the Old Testament, and the Old Testament itself gained a new vitality and relevancy because it had been fulfilled.

In a word, the New Testament writers believed that, in events which had taken place in their own time and under their own notice, the Old Testament had been fulfilled. This meant that, to some extent, an Old Testament interpretation was stamped upon the historical events; no New Testament writer questions that the Old Testament category of Messiahship is that in which the significance of Jesus must first be expressed. But to a far greater extent, the events imprinted their meaning upon the Old Testament, which henceforth could never be understood without reference to Jesus Christ.

It is this unique interplay of prophecy and event that makes up the Old Testament substructure of the New Testament. The Old Testament is fulfilled in the life, death, and resurrection of Jesus; but the fulfilment is determined by that which fulfils, not by that which is fulfilled. It is on this basis and on these terms that the Old Testament enters into the New.

We turn now to the second part of this lecture. The Bible in the New Testament period directs us first to that part of the Bible that was then complete, and we have examined the influence of the Old Testament upon the New Testament writers, and others; it directs us secondly to that part of the Bible that was then in process of becoming, to the New Testament in its embryonic form.

Before the Old Testament reached the form in which Jesus and his disciples knew it, parts of it at least had been handed down for centuries in oral tradition. The pre-literary, traditional stage of the New Testament was much shorter, but it was a period of great importance.

When we speak of tradition in relation to the New Testament, we mean that body of oral material which was eventually to crystallize into literary form in the New Testament itself. But this general definition requires further analysis.

First, there is the historical tradition which conveys information about what happened in the ministry of Jesus. It may be subdivided into the tradition of his teaching, and the narrative tradition of his deeds, but it is impossible to separate the two completely. There is no need here to discuss the historical value of these traditions; whenever and wherever they originated they certainly did exist before written gospels appeared.

So far the tradition has provided the materials for an informal biography of Jesus; but biography was not the primary interest of the primitive Church, which lived not by historical reminiscence but by the proclamation of the Gospel. In this proclamation too there existed a tradition. One of the most important results of the biblical study of the last quarter of a century has been the recognition [1] that the primitive preaching, as it may be studied in Acts, the Pauline Epistles, and elsewhere, follows a regular pattern. There was what may be called a kerygmatic tradition, which was in fact a primitive theology, as well as a biographical tradition.

Finally, there was an ecclesiastical and liturgical tradition. By this I mean a tradition that regulated the life, especially the ethical life, of the Church, and determined its behaviour in its common acts. Within this tradition were, for example, the household rules, which appear in similar form in several epistles (e.g., Col. 3. 18–4. 1), and Paul's account—one of the most clearly traditional parts of the New Testament—of what the Lord said and did in the night in which he was betrayed, a narrative Paul cites in order to correct disorders and abuses in the Corinthian Church (1 Cor. 11. 17–34).

Thus there were biographical tradition; kerygmatic tradition; and ecclesiastical and liturgical tradition.

These three forms of tradition may be distinguished, but it is impossible to hold them apart. The historical tradition cannot be separated from the other forms of tradition that were current in the early Church. It has been suggested that it was separate; that Jesus made his disciples learn his teaching by heart, and, as part of his teaching, his interpretation of the major events of his life. This view is difficult to maintain. References to the teaching of Jesus occur, though infrequently, in the epistles, but when they occur they are generally anonymous, and worked into the main thread of argument. We may cite, for example,

---

[1] See especially C. H. Dodd, *The Apostolic Preaching and its Developments*, 1936, where the *kerygma*, or preaching, of the New Testament period is analysed.

Paul's reference in Rom. 13 to the supreme law of love in which all other commandments are summed up. It is very unlikely that he is here independent of the teaching of Jesus (in Mark 12. 29ff and parallels) which is couched in almost identical terms; but he makes no attempt to cause this dominical material, this tradition of the sayings of Jesus, to stand out from his own instruction and exhortation.

As another example of the way in which the different strands of tradition were intertwined in the New Testament period we may note the frequency with which so-called "community rules" appear in the synoptic tradition. I pass no judgement here upon their historicity. It makes no difference to the present argument whether they are genuine recollections of words uttered by Jesus and subsequently applied to the needs of the Christian communities, or are the creation of the communities, made up by themselves for their own use. It is well known that widely different views have been held on this question. All that we need observe is the confluence of the "ecclesiastical" tradition, which contained the Church's rules, and the historical tradition, which offered biographical material about Jesus.

The most important question, however, both for our present study of the development of the New Testament in its pre-literary stage, and for the understanding of the origins of Christianity at large, is that of the relation between the historical tradition and the kerygmatic tradition, between the stories about Jesus and the primitive theological thinking and preaching of the early Church. I may illustrate the issue that is raised here by referring briefly to two different views.

Rudolf Bultmann begins his New Testament Theology with the sentence, "The preaching of Jesus belongs to the presuppositions of the theology of the New Testament, and is not itself a part of that theology."[1] He expresses the same point of view when in his book *Primitive Christianity in its Contemporary Setting* he places his paragraph "The Eschatological Preaching

[1] *Theologie des Neuen Testaments*, 1948–53, p. 1.

of Jesus" in the chapter headed "Judaism" and not in that headed "Primitive Christianity". The *kerygma* which represented Jesus Christ, crucified and risen, as God's eschatological act of salvation, arose after, not before, his death, though it has been read back into the historical tradition, so that it appears from time to time in the Gospels. In a word, "Jesus proclaimed the message. The Church proclaims *him*."[1] The effect of this judgement is to draw a clear line between the historical preaching of Jesus, and the historical preaching of the Church. In the course of time each came to affect the other, and the *kerygma* always looked back to the historical Jesus, but it gave to him a significance which he did not give to himself.

Oscar Cullmann views the matter differently. "The foundation of all Christology is the *life of Jesus*";[2] and this of course we can know only through the historical tradition. We are obliged to start with the life of Jesus, not only because the question who Jesus was was already raised in the minds of those who observed his ministry, but because he himself was conscious that it was through him that God was fulfilling his purpose, that he was the Son of man who would usher in the coming kingdom of God, and the Suffering Servant who by his death would gain forgiveness for mankind. When these themes appear in the Gospels, therefore, they do so not because the historical tradition has been contaminated by the theological, but because the historical tradition about Jesus already contained them.

I have set these two opinions over against each other because they are widely regarded as alternatives between which we must choose. Either we accept the radical historical scepticism of Dr Bultmann and recognize a gulf between the historical Jesus and the Church's proclamation about him, or we follow the more conservative line of Dr Cullmann and see the Christological *kerygma* already present in germ in genuine traditions going back to the ministry of Jesus. I do not wish to become

[1] *Primitive Christianity in its Contemporary Setting* (English Translation, 1956), p. 93.
[2] *Die Christologie des Neuen Testaments*, 1957, p. 327.

impaled upon either horn of this dilemma; each alternative has its difficulties. It seems to me practically certain that Jesus did believe his own activities to be organically related to the eschatological deliverance planned by God for his people, and that he must have recognized that his criticism of Judaism could lead only to his rejection. If nevertheless he continued to believe that God would establish his kingdom, he must have looked beyond his rejection and suffering to a vindication at least of his mission, and how his mission could be vindicated without a vindication of his person it is difficult to see. All this seems to follow, not from a discussion of this or that incident, but from the belief that Jesus saw a special connection (which we need not here attempt to define) between himself and the coming of the kingdom.

To say this, however, is one thing, and to suppose that we can penetrate the messianic consciousness of our Lord is another. For to do this we should have to provide ourselves with a critical tool by means of which we could distinguish between the historical tradition and the kerygmatic tradition, precisely in the area where they overlap: and it is hard to know where such a tool can be found.[1]

The root of the *kerygma*, or theological tradition, about Jesus is not the historical tradition of words which he is supposed to have uttered, or of actions which he is supposed to have done; it is rather the simple fact of Jesus, viewed in relation to the eschatological crisis, which is the interpretative context in which all parts of the New Testament (even James is scarcely an exception) agree in placing the fact. We may look back to the earlier part of this lecture and describe the event of Jesus Christ as the personal fulfilment of the Old Testament.

The various strands of the New Testament tradition all look back to this event and in different ways interpret and apply it; it is through the event that they interpret and apply the Old

---

[1] Except where certain concepts can be clearly distinguished as so markedly Hellenistic that they cannot be thought of as part of our Lord's human (Palestinian) consciousness.

20

Testament. When this is recognized both their independence and their mutual relationship can be understood.

Jesus taught, and his teaching was recorded. It was however unlike the conventional teaching of the Rabbis in that it was often (though not always) directed not to the elucidation and application of the Old Testament, but to the affirmation that the fulfilment of the Old Testament was at hand. His actions, especially his exorcisms, bore witness to the same truth, namely that in him God was beginning to act decisively with a view to setting up his kingdom. Like the theological tradition, the historical tradition of the words and deeds of Jesus is thus rooted in the *event*, and it is worthwhile to note that it is sometimes its sheer historical accuracy, its recounting things that Jesus said and did simply because he said and did them, that leads to a measure of diffuseness, of failure to concentrate upon the focal point.[1]

The relation of what I have called the ecclesiastical and liturgical tradition to the event of Jesus Christ is not quite so clear, but it nevertheless exists. The essential meaning of baptism and the eucharist is that they repeatedly represent and effect the eschatological event in the life of the Church; and the ecclesiastical tradition, the regulation of the order and obedience of the Church's life, means the submission of each concrete situation to the authority of the Redeemer.

We are now in a position to take up two themes of great importance, which may bring this lecture to a close.

First, there is the question of authority. Scripture, as we understand it, has authority. The tradition was the raw material of scripture; what then was its authority, and where did this authority reside?

This is not a simple question because, as we have seen, the New Testament tradition is of more than one kind. When we

---

[1] It is characteristic of the Fourth Evangelist that he handles the earlier tradition with a single eye to this concentration, even though the process sometimes results in the obscuring or distorting of "history" in the narrow sense.

speak of the historical tradition, what do we mean by authority? A natural answer will be, the authority of this tradition lies in its accuracy, its historical trustworthiness. A moment's consideration, however, will show that if this is what authority means, our documents, and the tradition on which they are based, did not possess it. For authority is not the same thing as probability, and though it may sometimes, or often, be shown that the Gospels are probably correct in what they record, there is no authority in such historians' arguments—as all historians know. Who can distinguish with complete confidence between a historical statement that has led to a theological conviction, and one that has grown out of a theological conviction?

The authority of the historical tradition resides rather in the effectiveness with which it points to the central event, the personal fulfilment of the plan of God first made known in the Old Testament. In clearer terms, the authority of the gospel tradition does not consist in the adequacy of the biographical materials which the Gospels contain but in the clarity of the witness they bear to Jesus Christ.[1] It is by this standard that the gospel material is to be measured, and when this standard is employed the Gospels regain the authority which historical criticism as such might have appeared to strip from them.

The theological side of the tradition invites similar treatment. The authority felt to be inherent in the *kerygma* is well illustrated by Paul's words in Gal. 1. 8f: "Even if we or an angel from heaven should preach you a Gospel other than that which we preached to you, let him be anathema.... If anyone preach you a Gospel different from that which you received, let him be

---

[1] This conclusion was worked out in terms of modern study of the Gospels; but it is perhaps worth noting that it leads to a close parallel to words of Luther: "All the genuine books of Holy Writ agree in this, that one and all they preach and treat of Christ. This too is the true touchstone for testing all books, to see whether they treat of Christ or not, since all scripture witnesses to Christ (Rom. 3. 21) and St Paul desires not to know anything save Christ (1 Cor. 2. 2). Whatever does not teach Christ, that is not apostolic, though St Peter or St Paul taught it. Conversely, whatever preaches Christ, that were apostolic, though Judas, Annas, Pilate, and Herod had the doing of it" (*Preface to the Epistles of St James and St Jude*, 1522).

anathema." We are bound to ask, How can Paul be so sure that
he is right?

For answer we will turn to another Pauline passage.[1] Paul's
account of the acts of Jesus at supper "in the night in which he
was betrayed" is introduced by the words, "I received from the
Lord (ἀπὸ τοῦ κυρίου), that which I also handed on to you,
namely that the Lord Jesus. . . ." (1 Cor. 11. 23). The meaning
of "from the Lord" has been much discussed, but it surely means
neither, "I received directly from the Lord in a vision", nor,
"I received by a process of tradition, the starting-point of which
was the Lord." In some sense the tradition carried with it the
authority of the Lord. We may compare Rom. 10. 14 ("How
shall they call on him in whom they have not believed? How
shall they believe in him whom they have not heard? How shall
they hear without one to preach?"), which implies that to hear
a preacher of the Gospel is to hear Christ himself.

The authority of the *kerygma* lies not in the person who
preaches but in the clarity with which it points to the focus of
divine activity, namely Jesus Christ. This may be illustrated by
the summary of the *kerygma* contained in the chapter from
which I have just quoted. "If you confess with your mouth,
'Jesus is Lord', and believe in your heart, 'God raised him from
the dead', you will be saved" (Rom. 10. 9). It would be hard
to point more clearly, in so few words, to the sovereignty and
centrality of Jesus Christ, and to his place in God's eschatological
plan of salvation. This clarity of reference to Jesus Christ is
that in which the authority of the kerygmatic or theological
tradition consists. No New Testament writer makes the point
more clearly than John: "This is how you know the Spirit of
God: every spirit which confesses that Jesus Christ has come in
the flesh is of God; and every spirit which does not confess Jesus
is not of God" (1 John 4. 2f).

It could be shown that the ecclesiastical and liturgical tradition enshrined in the New Testament has the same authority.
Christian ethical teaching is governed not by general ethical

[1] See the discussion by Cullmann in *The Early Church*, 1956, pp. 67f.

theory but by the command of Jesus Christ; and the Church's life and worship are ordered not by considerations of what is sociologically or emotionally impressive, but by its witness to the life, death, and resurrection of Jesus Christ. The authority of the New Testament tradition is, quite simply, Jesus Christ the Lord.[1]

Our final theme can now be briefly handled. This course of lectures is designed to show the impact of the Bible upon generation after generation of Christian life. Each generation has found its own problems in the Bible, and it would be a mistake, and dishonest, to minimize these; but it would be a far greater error if we failed to recognize that, notwithstanding the problems, age after age has found in the Bible an ever-flowing stream of living water springing up into eternal life. Because we have begun our study with the Bible, and biblical tradition, *in the New Testament period*, we can understand why this is so. The authority and the vitality of the Bible do not lie in a mechanical historical trustworthiness, or in ready applicability to the thought-forms and philosophical presuppositions of any age. This means that they are free for every age; and the man who is willing to stand under the authority of Jesus Christ, to whom prophets and apostles bear witness, will find that he is indeed the Way, the Truth, and the Life.

[1] The points that have now been made provide the foundation on which the doctrine of the Canon of New Testament scripture, and the authority of the New Testament over against non-canonical tradition, must rest. But this is a theme that cannot be pursued on this occasion.

The Bible and the Greek Fathers

HENRY CHADWICK

In the present series of lectures we are considering the place which the Bible holds and has held in the life and thought of the Christian Church. Our interest in the past is substantially concerned with the present. We are asking how the Bible has been treated in ancient, medieval, and post-Reformation times not only because the ideas of dead Christians are in themselves interesting but also because we are looking for light upon our modern problems. These modern problems have been focused in the idea of Revelation, and especially in the relation between the affirmation, on the one hand, that through the records which comprise the Bible he who has ears to hear may hear the word of God, and the affirmation, on the other hand, that the authors of these documents were human, and that their writings must be assessed and examined, like all other documents, in the spirit of free inquiry. This question lurks behind certain texts of the second and third centuries. But the interest of the ancient Church did not lie as much as ours does in the problem of relating divine revelation and human freedom as that problem appears in respect of the media of God's self-disclosure. They were more concerned with two other questions, namely, the discovery of rules for the correct interpretation of the Bible and the relation between scripture and the tradition of the Church. In one form or another all three questions were present to their minds, but the context was different from that in which they have been debated in more recent times. The tension between scripture and tradition as criteria of doctrine is prominent in Irenaeus and Tertullian, and is found in virtually all Fathers who discuss norms of authority at all. But this question for them

25

was not set in the same context as that of post-Reformation times, and in consequence, though Irenaeus' language may be so read as to sound like Bellarmine or like a contemporary Protestant controversialist, we must be on our guard against assuming that the meaning is the same. The different context is important, and subtly alters the nature of what is being said. This also holds good for discussions about allegory and typological interpretation. Patristic debate about the right use of allegorical exegesis may do something to illuminate our modern debates, but we must beware of assuming identity of standpoint. The school of Antioch in the fourth and fifth centuries may seem surprisingly modern. It is easy to turn Theodore of Mopsuestia into the patron saint of Liberal Protestantism. But we must not let our hearts run away with our heads. When the apparent similarity is at its greatest, we need to be most cautious lest, in our effort to make these dry bones live, we clothe the dead with too much of our own flesh and blood. In short, it may be true (I think it is) that the Fathers being dead yet speak. It is equally true that though they speak they are also dead. No simple transference is possible. At the same time there is obvious continuity. We know ourselves as Christians to share their common faith in the one Lord of the universal Church. We have a right to expect that we shall learn more about the nature of our own problems by a patient historical examination of theirs.

We may begin with the place of the Old Testament in the Bible of the early Church. The first Christians were not aware of any radical discontinuity between the present and the past. God who at sundry times and in divers manners had spoken in time past to the fathers by the prophets had now in these last days spoken by his Son. It was one and the same God who had created the world, who had given the covenant of circumcision to Abraham and the Law to Moses on Sinai, who had inspired Isaiah, Jeremiah, and the prophets, and who had now uniquely acted for his people by sending the Messiah. There was complete continuity in the divine providential plan for his people. Because of this conviction the primitive Church, as several books of the

New Testament make clear, was racked by the fearful problem of the Jews' rejection of Christ. It could be explained by saying that the people had been led astray by politically compromised and compromising leaders, or, by discerning with St Paul, a design to bring in the Gentiles within the one commonwealth of God and so to recall the Jewish people to recognize the things that belonged to their peace. But in any event the failure of the Jewish people as a whole to respond to Christ's proclamation of the kingdom of God did not and could not mean that the Old Testament was abrogated. The new must be somehow in line with the old. Therefore, apart from a few dissenters, the early Church took for granted the inspiration of the prophets as writers who pointed forward to the event of Christ's coming and were therefore to be interpreted in the light of that event. St Paul's happy phrase that the Law was a schoolmaster to bring us to Christ exactly expresses this sense of grateful retrospect towards the sacred writings of Israel.

From the third chapter of the Epistle to the Galatians it was thenceforward certain that the Old Testament would retain its place as sacred scripture for the Christians. This position was challenged in the second century by Marcion on the grounds that new wine must not be put into old bottles, that the Christian gospel was wholly new and absolutely discontinuous with Judaism—in a word, that the Old Testament could in no meaningful sense be described as revelation. Christ's teaching (Marcion held) was not a reform within the Jewish tradition, but a protest against it. Marcion's anti-Semitic violence provoked an intense reaction in the Church, and the reverberations of the controversy are heard for more than two hundred years. The orthodox reply in Irenaeus and Origen takes essentially twofold shape. First they insist on certain correspondences between the Old and New Testaments, beginning from the images borrowed from the Old Testament by the New Testament writers such as the description of Christ as the second Adam. Irenaeus works out his entire theory of "recapitulation" as a development of this basic typological theme, and it has its pre-eminent place in his system largely because of its controversial, anti-Marcionite significance. The doctrine of recapitulation is in itself a substantial answer to the Marcionite rejection of the Old Testtament as revelation.

Irenaeus' second line of argument in defence of the Old Testament uses the idea of a progressive education of the human race. The gnostic argument began from the orthodox presupposition that the New Testament was superior to the Old. Something in the Christian faith, they insisted, was new. By implication the typological argument denied or obscured this newness of development. Yet Christ himself had said, "Many prophets and righteous men have desired to see the things that you see and have not seen them" (Matt. 13.17; cf. Luke 10.24). The text was much quoted in this context at this period. In face of this text it was hard not to admit an advance. Irenaeus explains this advance by the two analogies of physical growth and intellectual progress. Man is not a static creature; personal identity is compatible with change. Just as an individual advances in comprehension, so also the Old Testament is the story of the education of the race, proceeding slowly as we may think but at a pace which is divinely ordered in accordance with the capacities of the recipients.

Irenaeus even hovers on the brink of linking this process of progressive education with the unfolding of the nature of God as Father, Son, and Holy Spirit. And although he never goes so far as to think of three distinct stages of revelation, each representing an advance on its predecessor and rendering it antiquated and superseded (like Joachim and the Spiritual Franciscans, or those Cambridge scholars who divided history into ancient, medieval, and modern), we are not far from this in the theology of the contemporary Montanists of Phrygia with whom Irenaeus had some degree of sympathy. In another context Irenaeus—like Origen in many passages—speaks of revelation as occurring in the three stages of Old Testament, New Testament, and the full vision, face to face, which will be attained in the life of the world to come.

Irenaeus' doctrine may be more accurately described as progressive education, however, than as progressive revelation. He therefore has to devote much space to explaining moral difficulties in the Old Testament—the problem of reconciling with divine goodness the plagues of Egypt, the hardening of Pharaoh's heart, the spoiling of the Egyptians by stealing their jewels at the exodus, and the unedifying behaviour of the daughters of Lot, these four narratives being particular favourites with the gnostic controversialists. His concept of an educational advance is thus imposed upon him by the requirements of his defence of the faith. It is, as it were, superimposed upon his deeper and more instinctive view that revelation is timeless, standing above the historical process of change and decay, and that therefore the Old Testament and the New are not so much different stages in the apprehension of truth as complementary ways of expressing one and the same truth about God. According to the typological exegesis the Old Testament is wholly Christian if correctly interpreted. It expresses the same truth as the New Testament, only differing in its use of imagery and symbolism.

In practice Irenaeus is constantly interpreting his Old Testament by a given criterion, namely, that of the person of Christ. The Law and the prophets are theologically significant because they point forward to one greater than Solomon and Jonah. The exodus and the return from the exile by the waters of Babylon are events which manifest God's judgement and mercy and so illuminate and prefigure the nature of the redemptive love of God in Christ. In its essentials Irenaeus could have made his own the attitude of the Epistle to the Hebrews, that in the Law and the prophets God had made a partial revelation expressed in various forms through different writers; now he had summed it all up and brought it to its fulfilment and culmination in the Lord of history and of the Church.

The story of the emergence of the New Testament as a sacred collection side by side with the Old Testament is a large and fascinating subject, on which it is hardly possible to do more than touch here. The collection derives its existence in the last analysis from the sovereign authority of the Lord himself among his disciples. For the first generation of the Church the authority of Christ, in so far as it does not simply consist in his remembered words and actions, inheres in the chosen circle of apostolic witnesses. But the apostles died, and with the passing from the scene of those who had actually seen and heard the Lord the problem of authority became acute. One answer was to look to prophecy. The early Church included a number of prophets who might deliver inspired revelations of the risen Lord. But the standing of prophecy declines. There was the perennial difficulty of distinguishing true from false prophecy; and the "New Prophecy" of the Montanists brought all such utterances into disrepute. Visions and revelations were all very well, but if Christ were a full and final disclosure of God then no subsequent revelation could supplement or correct that which had already been given. The only prophecy to gain final admission to the New Testament canon was the Johannine Apocalypse. Beside the memory of Jesus' sayings and doings it was also possible to appeal to apostolic writings. The apostle Paul had written several letters to his churches in the exercise of his apostolic authority. It is clear that these letters were not written with any notion that one day they might form part of a canon of sacred scripture. Except for Romans and Ephesians they have an occasional character, and all are written in a particular, concrete situation. Nevertheless, these letters were written with authority. Indeed Paul found by experience that it was better to write, since he was more effective on paper than in person. "His letters" (said the malicious Corinthians) "are weighty and powerful, but his bodily presence is weak and his speech contemptible." A group of these letters came to be preserved (how this happened is a matter of speculation) and became an independent corpus, copied in a codex. We hear of Christians in the second and third centuries who possessed codices containing the Pauline epistles. One bishop of Asia Minor informs us in the inscription on his tombstone, which he wrote himself, that he had travelled about the Roman Empire from the Euphrates to Rome carrying a copy in his pocket.

Apostolic letters were, accordingly, one norm of authority for guiding the life and worship of the second-century communities. These letters, however, did not contain much direct information about the tradition of Jesus' teaching. The Gospels seem to have become established reading in church lectionaries in divers ways and divers manners. Some churches used one Gospel, some another. Then they exchanged texts, and gradually the independent Gospels were brought together. At first, of course, the word "gospel" meant the message, not the book, and this is reflected in the second-century titles. It was the one Gospel of Jesus Christ, whether according to Mark, or Matthew, or Luke, or John. There were four versions of the story, four portraits of its central figure. Beside the four "canonical" Gospels (to use an anachronistic phrase) the second century soon had other collections of Christ's sayings, like the recently discovered Gospel of Thomas, or the Gospel according to the Egyptians, or the Gospel according to the Hebrews, or the Gospel of Peter —and many others.

The Gospels were authoritative because they enshrined the tradition about Jesus. In the first half of the second century there is no sense of any antithesis between scripture and tradition. Scripture possesses authority because it is tradition: it represents the written part of the deposit handed down from the apostles. At first, it seems, its written character was not entirely appreciated. Papias observes that he especially endeavoured to question elderly Christians who had actually known the apostles, believing that he could catch more of the spirit of the faith from the living, oral tradition than from records in books. It must be admitted that what Papias managed to extract from this oral tradition does not look impressive.

Papias differentiates between oral and written tradition to disparage the latter. This could no longer be safely said after the main gnostic challenge had precipitated violent conflict over the nature of authentic Christianity. Marcion and Valentine arrived in Rome about 140; each claimed that his doctrine was the true faith and thereby denied the correctness or sufficiency of the doctrine being taught by the Roman clergy. It was good to be able to point in reply to the succession of occupants of the teaching chairs in which the martyred heroes St Peter and St Paul had once sat to instruct the Roman church. It was even better to be able to vindicate the proposition that the contemporary bishop and presbyters of Rome taught what the apostles had taught. It could be proved by written documents. The tradition was open to control in the words of scripture. The teaching of the apostles had providentially been put into writing, so that it was no matter of guesswork to ascertain its nature.

Marcion and Valentine were especially formidable because they could strike at this argument. They did so in two antithetical ways. Marcion, on the one hand, asserts that the documents have been corrupted by Judaizers, and sets about the complex task of producing the genuine, uninterpolated text. He makes a purified edition of the Pauline epistles, with the Epistle to the Galatians at its head to emphasize the apostle's hostility to Judaizing Christianity. He likewise expurgated St Luke's Gospel. Why he chose St Luke is not known, but the simplest explanation—that St Luke was a Gentile and the friend of St Paul—is probably right. The Acts, however, he rejected as a tendentious work, papering over the cracks of the radical cleavage between St Paul and the other, Judaizing apostles. St Luke's Gospel was the only authoritative Gospel. There could not be more than one authentic Gospel, and the orthodox notion that there might be more than one was a mere device for escaping difficulties. When pressed with arguments from the text of one, they took refuge in another. Accordingly Marcion is the first person of whom we know that he produced a rigidly determined text and canon of the New Testament. (The Old Testament he rejected entirely.)

Valentine, Basilides, and other heretics of the mid-second century, answered the orthodox argument not by subtracting from their canon of scripture like Marcion but by adding to it.

They fully accepted the authority of the apostolic writings, but they produced, like rabbits out of a hat, additional sources of very unexpected theological information. They had secret books or "apocrypha", containing records of the esoteric teaching given by Jesus to his disciples. They also claimed to have access to yet more confidential information in an oral tradition, so mysterious that it could not even be committed to writing at all, describing the teaching given by Jesus to the apostles during the forty days after his resurrection. With this key they could unlock the mysteries of Christ's parables; they had the interpretation expounded to the disciples secretly (cf. Matt. 13. 36).

It was now urgent to fix the canon and that right speedily. The essential test was apostolicity. These apocryphal documents must be excluded. But it was not easy to be sure about these problems of authenticity. How did one know that the Gospel of Peter was not really by Peter? As late as the end of the second century this problem provided harassing difficulties for the bishop of Antioch, Serapion, who visited the Syrian town of Rhosus and found them rent by a dispute. The issue turned out to be whether or not the Gospel of Peter might be read publicly in the lectionary. Serapion, not suspecting the presence of heresy in the community, said that of course the work of an apostle might be read. But subsequent study of the work revealed to him that he had been hasty; the work was heretical, therefore it could not be apostolic. The episode perfectly illustrates the difficulties of the second-century Church. The scripture could only be proved genuine by its orthodoxy—in other words, by its correspondence with the traditional doctrine of the Church. The Bible had once been called in to vindicate the authenticity of the tradition. It now had to be vindicated by that tradition. The circle was complete.

The consequence of the virtual equation of apostolicity with orthodoxy meant the eventual exclusion of orthodox works like the so-called "First" Epistle of Clement which did not claim to be apostolic, and the inclusion of writings like the Second

Epistle of Peter which claimed to be apostolic and could not readily be detected as being anything else because they were orthodox. The heretical pseudepigraphon presented fewer problems than the orthodox production of the same type of article. It was not too difficult to discern the heretical tendencies of the Gospel of Peter, and Serapion of Antioch explains that he only failed to realize the truth in the first place because he had not studied the document in question. Once he had examined it, its heretical nature was clear to him. But the orthodox pseudepigraphon was not detectable by the same texts. Litmus paper did not change colour in its presence.

A decisive factor in determining the meaning of "orthodoxy" in this context was provided by the weight of precedent in the various churches, particular regard being paid to churches of apostolic foundation. The churches had long been reading the gospels and the epistles in their lectionary and also in private Bible study at home apart from the corporate worship of the community. Questions of authenticity could therefore be settled quickly by arguing from the general consensus of Christian custom, which was a method much more practicable than any appeal to expert or scholarly opinion, even if such an opinion had been forthcoming.

This authority of usage and precedent saved the position of the second and third gospels which were not associated with an apostolic name. They could, however, be given protection by being placed under the umbrella of St Peter and St Paul respectively. But the argument from precedent was strong, and so already existing custom did much to modify the way in which the criterion of apostolicity was applied. There is a sense in which the idea of the New Testament canon was created overnight by the magnitude of the gnostic crisis. In churches like Rome where the impact of heresy was sharpest, the idea of prescribing a fixed number of received books was no gradual growth. It was an urgent, immediate answer to a problem that brooked no delay. But not all churches were affected to the same degree. The gravity of the situation varied greatly from one community to another, and this variation meant that there was no general co-ordination on the point among the churches. Only local councils met in the second or even in the third century to determine the limits of the canon. Authoritative directives from the great sees first appear in the second half of the fourth century. Accordingly while the criteria for admission to the sacred writings were agreed in the second century and never modified, yet there was much variation, for a length of time which appears astonishing, about the manner in which these criteria were applied. There were disagreements about the precise status of certain books for centuries. This fact astonishes us, however, because we look back at the ancient Church through modern spectacles. The really surprising thing is the degree of unanimity achieved so rapidly by the very diverse and scattered congregations throughout the Mediterranean world from Britain to Mesopotamia. Moreover, the force of local conservatism made for variation. The First Epistle of Clement was still being read in the lectionary of many churches in the fourth century. The Shepherd of Hermas, eliminated from Rome's lectionary during the second century, persisted in that of Alexandria until the fourth.

It was the crisis of the second century which led to the formation of the New Testament as a closed canon. Of the benefits of this development there can be no doubt. Nevertheless the effect of the crisis was to make the relation between scripture and tradition problematic and bedevilled by ambiguities and unresolved questions. For instance, in the middle of the second century it would not seem as evident as it does to us that the teaching of the apostles was limited to that contained in their writings. It was still reasonable to suppose that there could be some oral tradition of what they had said. Papias in Asia Minor was still able to consult people who could claim, rightly or wrongly but at any rate plausibly, to have conversed with apostles and therefore to give a specially authoritative account of their "interpretations" of the Lord's sayings. Furthermore, there was an age-old prejudice, widespread in the ancient

D

world, against committing the profounder truths to writing. Traces of this esotericism may be found even within the New Testament itself. To claim that all truth had been put into publicly accessible books was to invite the accusation that the Christians either had nothing profound to say or that they were vulgarly revealing delicate and deep truths which any sensitive soul would instinctively wish to keep from the madding crowd. Again, the letters of St Paul were obviously occasional writings, designed to meet specific questions in particular churches, or addressed to individual friends like Philemon. Were they intended to convey timeless truths of revelation? And were all his letters inspired? Could he put pen to paper without being inspired? If all his letters to his churches were inspired, why do the surviving letters show that some have been lost? I Corinthians 5. 9 mentions a lost letter to Corinth, Colossians 4. 16 a letter from Laodicea. Could God have allowed his timeless revelations by inspired letters to become lost? Surely divine providence might be expected to take better care than that of documents given to instruct the human race in the way of salvation.

These questions are all raised at this period, and show the problems which resulted from the formation of the canon. That the creation of the canon was of immense benefit in providing a control upon doctrinal development is evident. And the Bible remains the supreme norm of authority for all the Fathers, both Greek and Latin, so that it was never possible for any further norms of authority, such as creeds and conciliar pronouncements, to be regarded as other than interpretative safeguards for the true tradition of orthodoxy enshrined in the plain text of scripture itself. Nevertheless, the concept of the closed canon made for difficulties.

In the first place it put the apostolic age on a pedestal. It made people think of it as a golden age when apostolic zeal and unity were rewarded by signs and wonders and manifestations of the Holy Spirit, in a manner utterly remote from the discord, intrigue, and extremely unmiraculous Church life of the second and third centuries. It was as if the apostolic age corresponded to the state of Adam and Eve before the Fall, with Simon Magus to play the rôle of Cain as the first villain to introduce heresy into the Church, hitherto preserved without spot or wrinkle or any such thing. In consequence, the Church has ever since felt itself to be endeavouring, like the Sun-bathing Association, to recover lost innocence.

In the second place it obscured the diversity and spontaneity of the biblical writings. The identification of the primary witness to God's revelation in Christ with a rigidly determined book made Christians treat the Bible as if it were a Koran, a volume that had been given at divine dictation, every part being from a single divine author and therefore of equal value and significance. Among the Greek Fathers this tendency was accentuated by the influence of Philo upon Clement of Alexandria and Origen. Philo treated the Pentateuch as a divine cryptogram which could be solved by special inspiration and by close attention to the etymology of Hebrew proper names, to number-mysticism, and to oddities of sense and syntax which the ingenious Moses had carefully inserted in the text to act as clues to the puzzle. Philo was gratefully transcribed not only by Clement and Origen, but also by Ambrose so that his methods passed to the West.

In the second and third centuries the Church was the scene of impassioned debate about the problem of historical difficulties in scripture. The Mosaic authorship of the Pentateuch, the date of the Book of Daniel, the credibility of the story of Jonah, the dimensions of Noah's Ark, the discrepancies among the evangelists in respect of the placing of the cleansing of the Temple—these and many like questions were keenly discussed. A disciple of Marcion named Apelles remarked that if the Ark really had been of the size stated in Genesis it could only have contained four elephants and their food. Origen rather weakly replied that everything is all right provided that you square the measurements. The literal sense is thereby saved. But for Origen the Ark is really a symbol of the Church in which men of reason are a minority—he would have happily agreed with the memorable judgement of Warburton: "The Church, like the Ark of Noah, is worth saving; not for the sake of the unclean beasts and vermin that almost filled it, and probably made most noise and clamour in it, but for the little corner of rationality, that was as much distressed by the stink within as by the tempest without."

In truth, Origen was always glad of a difficulty or a contradiction, since it proved that one must interpret allegorically; the interpreter must rise from the letter that kills to the spirit that gives life, which for Origen means rising from the historical level of space and time to the eternal and transcendent order, from the realm of the body to the realm of the soul. Just as Christ's body has no beauty to those down below in the valley but is transfigured to the disciples who ascend the Mount, so also the garments of the Word in scripture become radiant to his saints.

Origen tries hard to meet the charge that his allegories are pure subjectivism. We are not likely to be very impressed by the arguments which he uses to establish their objectivity. But his final justification lies, perhaps, in the fact that by allegory he is able to make scripture contemporary, more than a remote record of the distant past. He could also appeal to authority in the evident precedent of St Paul and the clear use of symbolism in St John's Gospel.

The Antiochene exegetes of the following century were much more historical and literalistic in their exegesis. It is significant that, as Mr Wiles has observed in his recent book *The Spiritual Gospel*, they were not much at home with St John. Moreover, as we learn from St John Chrysostom, congregations did not always think that they derived much spiritual benefit from discourses about the date and order of St Paul's epistles. Whatever dangers might attach to allegory, at least it was one of its merits that it was akin to poetic fancy. Augustine somewhere observes that a truth will often go home to a congregation when their imagination is stimulated by a fanciful piece of allegorical exegesis. They remain unmoved by plain prose.

To conclude, the story is one of both loss and gain. Apologetic necessities and the quest for religious certainty led some of the Greek Fathers to make too absolute an identification of the Bible with revelation. I have tried to describe a few of the difficulties in which they consequently found themselves. Nevertheless, in the main it is true to say this much on the positive side. They did not lose sight of the fundamental point that Christianity is the religion not of a book but of a Person, that the Bible has its unique and irreplaceable authority in the Church because the prophets and apostles bear witness to him. They were aware—you may think too much aware—that literal and historical truth is not the only kind of truth. And they were aware that, whatever particular problems may arise, the Bible needs to be taken as a whole, and that its significance for faith is bound up with the total context of the Church's continuous life and worship.

The Bible and the Latin Fathers

J. N. D. KELLY

IT IS understandable that a student investigating the use of
the Bible in the early Church should prepare himself for a
feeling of disappointment, of anticlimax at least, when he turns
from the East to the West. He is moving, he knows in advance,
from a richly stocked, amazingly luxuriant garden to one that is
more homely in style and more sparsely planted. Christian
Latin literature hardly begins before Tertullian, and how
meagre is the company of Latin writers between him and Leo
the Great as compared with the army of Greeks! If the terrain
is thus more manageable, a good deal of it has been traversed
already and is bound to be familiar, for a common tradition of
exegesis, certain accepted presuppositions about the Bible as an
inspired book, pervaded Christendom as a whole in the
patristic age. Moreover, it was the Greeks, we all know, who
were the brilliant improvisors and innovators in this field, while
the Latin Fathers, including some of the most illustrious, were
all too often content with the rôle of imitators and borrowers.

These suspicions obviously contain a large element of truth,
but it would be unfortunate if our student, still more unfortunate if we ourselves, were to be deterred by them from
continuing his, or our, explorations. The Latin Fathers, it is
agreed, made a weighty, and also a distinctive, contribution to
theology, and it was based almost entirely on their understanding of the biblical revelation. They were, if anything, even
more Bible-minded than their Greek counterparts for the
reason that, except for an odd man out like Marius Victorinus
and a genius like Augustine, they had little taste, and even less
capacity, for philosophical speculation. We should scarcely be

surprised to find, therefore, that, for all their copying of Greek models, their approach to the Bible and their methods of handling it occasionally reveal an original quality which can fairly be described as Latin, and which may even, to some extent at any rate, account for the differences of emphasis between Latin and Greek theology. Further, the fact that the Latin scene is much less crowded than the Greek offers certain practical advantages. At the very least, the trees are not so numerous as to prevent one from seeing the wood, and one is therefore better placed for assessing the character and value of the ancient Fathers' use of Scripture.

If then we are reconciled to our subject, we shall best come to grips with it if we select several key-aspects and examine each of them separately. We may usefully begin by inquiring what exactly the Latin Fathers understood by the Bible. In effect this is to raise the question of the canon, which happens to be one of the departments in which the West made a definite contribution and followed a distinctive line of its own. As regards the Old Testament this can be illustrated by their attitude to the Apocrypha, or deutero-canonical books. The vacillations of the East in this matter are well known, and to be honest, do it credit. At first the Apocrypha was treated without question as Scripture, but once well informed students like Origen became aware of the discrepancy between the Hebrew and Alexandrian canons, doubts crept in. The theoretical conclusion of the great fourth-century Eastern Fathers (their actual practice was often at variance with it) was that the deutero-canonical books should be relegated to a subordinate position outside the canon proper. The West, on the contrary, seems never to have wavered in its view that they had every right to be included in the Bible. Jerome, it is true, influenced by his long residence in Palestine as well as by scholarly considerations, took the Eastern line, as did his *bête-noire*, Rufinus. These were isolated protesters, however, and Augustine's definition of the Old Testament as consisting of forty-four books and his refusal to distinguish between the Apocrypha and the rest represented the characteristic Western position.

When we turn to the New Testament, the chief point to note is that the West seems to have been responsible both for the idea of a canon of Christian scriptures and for the creation of the earliest such canons. The Roman passion for law and order, for tidiness and protocol, may have had something to do with it, but the immediate stimulus came from Marcion, who, working apparently with Rome as his centre, published his own highly selective, bowdlerized list in the forties of the second century. He has sometimes been acclaimed as the creator of the catholic canon, but that is of course an exaggeration. The Church already possessed its roughly defined collection, or, rather, collections, of Christian writings which it was beginning to treat as Scripture. Before Marcion, however, none of the great ecclesiastical centres, so far as we know, had formally defined which books, and which alone, were to be regarded as such. His action (the influence of Montanism worked in the same direction) made it imperative to take precisely this step, and there is evidence that official canons began to be drawn up in the West in the latter part of the second century. The so-called Muratorian fragment, the earliest extant ecclesiastically authorized list of New Testament books, is one of these, and is of course directly connected with Rome.

Secondly, not only was the West earlier in the field in prescribing a fixed canon, but it showed considerable independence of the East in its choice of books. This is not the place to set out the complicated story in detail, but we should remind ourselves of its outlines. On the one hand, the West remained untouched by the fierce debate about the canonicity of Revelation which raged in the East. On the other, the West took a much stiffer line from the start with books like Hermas and the Apocalypse of Peter which in the East hovered on the fringe of the canon for centuries; it also showed great reluctance to admit Hebrews and the Catholic Epistles apart from I Peter and I John. Its doubts about the former were dictated by the absence of any indication of apostolic authorship, and some may be inclined to regret that its objections to the minor epistles did not prevail. In any case recognition was accorded to them all towards the end of the fourth century, but it needed the strenuous efforts of popes supported by theologians like Jerome and Augustine to secure this; and it is plain that the governing motive was the desire not to be out of step with the Greek Church.

The next aspect at which I would invite you to glance is the inspiration of Scripture. In spite of its central importance, there is no need to spend much time on this subject, for the ideas of the Latin Fathers were neither original nor of any special interest. Like all ancient Christians, they took it for granted that the Bible was inspired; God was its author, and the writers of the several books were his instruments. Moreover, it was inspired—equally inspired, if the expression is permissible— in all its parts, so that Augustine could affirm that the very titles of the Psalms were divinely ordered, and Jerome could discern a supernatural import in every minutest detail of Philemon. By inspiration they meant the direct influence of the Holy Spirit on the minds and wills of the sacred writers. This influence was not understood as being akin to ecstasy or possession. Such a theory had been held by Philo, and was eagerly embraced by the Montanists (including Tertullian when he joined that movement), but the orthodox tradition was careful to emphasize that there was no resemblance whatever between the inspired writers, whose condition had been perfectly normal, and the ecstatic oracles of paganism. Hippolytus, for example, explained that when the Word moved the prophets the effect was simply to clarify their vision and instruct their understanding; while Jerome pointed out that they retained the full, normal use of their faculties, and also made much of the differences of style, general culture, and background their works exhibited. Augustine argued that in compiling the Gospels the evangelists had relied on their own reminiscences, the function of the Holy Spirit being to arouse their memories and preserve them from making mistakes. The net result was that there could be no error of any kind anywhere in Scripture. Augustine had a crushing retort to anyone so rash as to surmise the presence of one: *aut codex mendosus est, aut interpres erravit, aut tu non intelligis*.

All this is commonplace stuff really, with plenty of parallels in the East; but I suspect that it leaves most modern readers with an uneasy, dissatisfied feeling. Quite apart from the awkward implications of the doctrine of verbal inerrancy, the assumption that the whole of Scripture is uniformly inspired hardly seems to distinguish between the utterance of the prophet consciously declaring the word of the Lord and the plain narrative of the historian. Our Latin Fathers whole-heartedly accepted this; and we have it on Jerome's authority that, even when St Paul frankly disclaimed having received any revelation, as when he was giving advice about virgins, he was nevertheless divinely inspired. Again, while Augustine was clearly interested in the problem of the mode of the Spirit's operation and liked to speculate about the various types of vision (corporal, spiritual, and intellectual) which God employed to communicate divine truths to the sacred authors, his analyses do not take us very far. A more searching question is whether, by virtually limiting it to inspiration in the sense defined, these early Latin Fathers were not making use of much too narrow and one-sided a conception of revelation. In Hippolytus, a profounder thinker than many in the West, we catch occasional hints of a more comprehensive view of the function of the Logos in revelation, but those who came after him did not follow these up. Only towards the end of our period did Augustine adumbrate, in his *De civitate Dei*, a view of history as the field of God's self-disclosure and judgement; but he made little or no attempt to link these reflections with his elucidation of the biblical message.

We must next inquire how the Latin Fathers conceived of the relation of the Old Testament to the New. This was, as everyone knows, a fundamental issue in the early Church, and unless it was settled aright the true significance of the biblical revelation was in danger of being misapprehended. The basic principles were worked out extremely early, indeed at the New Testament stage, and for their ultimate warrant we must look to our Lord's application of Old Testament ideas and motifs to his own mission. The solution adopted was the assumption that the key-personages and events of the old dispensation could be regarded as types, that is, as anticipating and prefiguring, the personages and events of the new; and the underlying premiss was that history, especially the history of Israel, was the scene of the progressive unfolding of God's redemptive purpose. I need only refer you to C. H. Dodd's *According to the Scriptures* for a fairly recent examination, as suggestive as it is fresh, of the methods which were employed in the primitive Church to demonstrate the correspondence between the two Testaments.

The pioneer work in this field had been accomplished before the dawn of Christian Latin literature. Even so, Tertullian's discussion of the Christian relevance of the Old Testament, contained notably in his *Adversus Marcionem*, remains an impressive example of the earlier form of this apologetic—the kinship between this work and Justin's Dialogue with Trypho is striking. His object is to prove, Bible in hand, to his Marcionite antagonists that Jesus, the Christ of the New Testament, is identical with the Messiah of the prophets. So he ransacks the Old Testament for passages which seem to predict the kind of spiritual reign which Christ has in fact established, or which seem to foreshadow his birth, passion, and resurrection, or which represent the character of the Messiah as resembling our Lord's, or which anticipate the rejection of the Jews and the call of the Gentiles. The detail of his argument would not carry conviction even in conservative circles to-day, but every Christian must recognize the importance of the central truth for which he was contending, and most of us would be prepared to agree that his claim, as against the Marcionites, that Christ was the fulfilment of the hope of Israel was well founded.

This old-fashioned method of picking out selected passages of the Old Testament—often arranged as proof texts, but in fact (as Dr Dodd has argued) consisting of large sections which were understood as wholes—and showing how they pointed forward to the gospel story continued long in vogue in the West. For examples we need only refer to Cyprian's *Testimonia* and Ambrosiaster's *Quaestiones veteris et novi testamenti*. On the other hand, Christians in the West no less than the East were anxious to make profitable spiritual use of those much larger portions of the Old Testament which did not have an ostensibly messianic bearing. With their unhistorical approach they could not attribute to them any value in their own right, and had not the Apostle insisted that when the Almighty legislated about cattle in the Old Testament he was not really concerned about cattle but about us? Hence there spread to the West the custom of regarding the whole Old Testament, and not just decisive segments of it, as pregnant with Christian significance. Early examples from Rome are the two commentaries by Hippolytus on the Song of Songs and Daniel respectively. In the latter, which covers the story of Susanna and the elders, Hippolytus claims that Susanna and her husband really signify the Church and Christ; the garden of Joakim is the place where God plants his elect, who are trees laden with rich fruits; the two lustful old men are the two groups of Jews and Gentiles who are united in savage assault against the Church; Susanna's bath symbolizes the waters of baptism, while the two servants assisting her are faith and charity. One could carry on endlessly; once one has set out on this path, the only limits are those set by one's mental dexterity, the fecundity of one's imagination— and what the pious reader will stand.

It is plain that this kind of approach, however edifying, hopelessly obscured the true relationship (at least, what we are bound to regard as the true relationship) of the Old to the New Testament. Yet it was destined to be tremendously popular in the West. Ambrose exploited it to the full, as did his earlier contemporary, Hilary. The latter, both in his exposition of the

47

Psalms and in his *Tractatus mysteriorum*, laid it down that the Old Testament is *in its entirety* prefigurative of the New. For example, each psalm has its own special key, and he who would explore its meaning must first get possession of this (he borrowed the idea from Origen); but faith in Jesus Christ is in any case the universal pass-key which unlocks all the mysteries of the Old Testament. It was Tyconius, however, the Donatist exegete of the second half of the fourth century, who gave formal shape to these principles in his celebrated *Liber regularum*. In the first two of his seven rules he insisted that the Old Testament was in all its parts the figure or symbol of the New. The devout reader was entitled to refer every single text in these Jewish books which the Christians had inherited either to Christ and his Church or to the devil and his disciples. Tyconius' theory made an enormous impression on his contemporaries. Augustine in particular took it over lock, stock, and barrel, and it was in this sense that he formulated his famous epigram, *In vetere testamento novum latet, et in novo vetus patet*.

From the problem of the Old Testament we turn naturally to the theory and practice of exegesis which prevailed in the West. Here we are justified, I think, in making a fairly clear distinction between what I should like to call the authentically Latin approach and an approach which, though widely used by the Latin Fathers, was essentially an importation from without. The exponents of the former anticipated, or at any rate were working on parallel lines with, the Antiochene school, although they did not like it construct a theoretical basis for their method. The characteristic of the latter was to attach chief importance to the so-called spiritual sense, to make lavish and often indiscriminate use of allegory, and in a word to place Origen on a pedestal as their admired master and model.

We can cite Tertullian, Ambrosiaster, and Jerome as illustrations, all three important and all three very different, of the literal school of interpretation. Sporadic references to Tertullian's principles can be found up and down his works. The

Bible reader should advance, he argued, from the known to the unknown, from the more to the less sure; he should seek light for dark passages from the mass of clear ones. What mattered was not the words themselves but the meaning behind them. Doubtful contexts in the Old Testament should be cleared up by reference to the New, since Christ was the fulfilment of prophecy. His ideal was to read the Bible in as straightforward a way as possible, reducing allegory to a minimum. He admitted readily enough that figurative language was the prophet's stock-in-trade; but he pointed out that, so far from dispensing with reality, it ought to presuppose it. For example, even if one takes the eschatological prophecies symbolically, the end of the world nevertheless remains a truth foretold by Scripture. Unless care was exercised, however, there was danger of so using allegory as to dissolve Bible truth into thin air. This applied particularly to the physical resurrection, which could only be interpreted in a purely spiritual sense at the cost of evacuating the texts of their plain meaning; and of course to our Lord's teaching. It was an error, for example, to seek symbolical explanations of all the minute details of the parables; most of them are decoration, *mise en scène*, and concentration on them distracts one from what is essential. Again, the Gospel contains absolutely categorical statements about the judgement, the kingdom of God, and the resurrection which must be taken *ut sonant* without vainly hunting for symbols.

The problem of the identity of Ambrosiaster, the enigmatic contemporary of Pope Damasus (366–84) who wrote a famous commentary on St Paul's epistles and also the pseudo-Augustinian *Quaestiones veteris et novi testamenti*, has never been solved, but he remains a vitally important witness to the Pauline text used at Rome prior to Jerome and to the pre-Augustinian understanding of the Apostle. As a student of Scripture his chief weakness, oddly enough, was his casual attitude to the Greek original and his uncritical partiality for the Latin version. He was aware, for example, that in Greek Rom. 5. 14 reads the direct opposite of the Latin *et in eos qui peccaverunt in simili-*

49

tudinem praevaricationis, but he stubbornly stuck to the latter for reasons which even in his own day ought not to have borne scrutiny. The practical effects of this blind-spot were, however, not very far-reaching, and in general his handling of Scripture was extremely conscientious and sensible. His object was always to bring out the historical and literal meaning to the best of his ability, and he liked to press the Apostle's message home to his readers by means of practical illustrations drawn from familiar situations. In the main he avoided allegorical and symbolical interpretations, although he was occasionally driven to them (e.g. when explaining certain Old Testament texts, or when spiritualizing the imagery describing the joys of the millenium). No one would claim that he brought to the thought of St Paul the insight of an Augustine, a Luther, or a Calvin; but we can still admire his honest, straightforward attempt to comprehend the text before him.

At first sight Jerome, generally reckoned the greatest Latin exegete, might seem out of place in this company of literalist Bible readers. In interpreting Scripture he adopted Origen's distinction of three senses, although in practice he usually confined himself to the literal or historical sense and the spiritual sense. In his earlier period his enthusiasm for the latter carried him away, and he even wrote a youthful commentary on Obadiah, later to be disavowed, which was allegorical through and through and wholly ignored the historical element. At this phase he spoke disparagingly of *vilis intelligentia secundum litteram, humilitas litterae, carnalis intelligentia*, etc. What particularly attracted him to the spiritual sense was the wonderfully easy, and at the same time edifying, way in which it enabled the devout Christian to deal with the anthropomorphisms, apparent inconsistencies, improprieties, and other awkwardnesses of which the Bible was embarrassingly full. From 393 or 394, however, that is, from the outbreak of his campaign against Origenism, a remarkable change began to come over his theory and practice. About 398, for example, we find him producing a commentary on Isaiah 13–23 which made a serious attempt to be historical; again, in his commentary on Matthew, which belongs to the same time, his chief concern was to bring out the historical content of the Gospel. He never lost his preference for the spiritual sense; but he came increasingly to realize that, if it was to escape being arbitrary, capricious, and purely subjective, it must be solidly grounded in the literal sense. There can be no doubt that Jerome's ever-deepening studies in the text and original languages of the Bible, and his intimate acquaintance with the Holy Land where the sacred history had been enacted, played a great part in this development of his exegetical ideas.

We can deal more briefly with the representatives of the allegorical or spiritualizing school of exegesis, for although their influence was the more dominant they themselves had little originality and were largely dependent on Eastern models. I have already mentioned Hippolytus; here I need only add that, if he gave full rein to his allegorical fancy in his commentaries on Daniel and Song of Songs, his purely theological exegesis, as exhibited in his treatise against Noetus, was more sober in style and closely resembled that of Tertullian. Towards the end of the third century the allegorical method found another champion in the first Latin-writing exegete, the uncouth stylist Victorinus of Pettau (d. 304), who although a strict literalist in interpreting the millenarian texts of the Apocalypse took Origen as his master in exegesis. It was in the middle and second half of the fourth century, however, that this method really came into its own in the West, when it was taken up by theologians of the calibre and prestige of Hilary and Ambrose. The former employed it lavishly even in his commentary on Matthew, being enabled by it to deduce (to give you a by no means untypical sample of his reasoning) that the deeper motive for our Lord's teaching from a ship on a certain famous occasion was to indicate that his word was only truly preached and understood in the Church, symbolized by the ship. Ambrose undoubtedly was the most brilliant and consistent exponent of the method, and we all remember the impression his use of it made on Augustine at a critical phase of his religious development. He borrowed his principles directly from Philo and Origen, of whom he was a close student, and indeed was indebted to them for the detail of his interpretations as well. It was his theory that there was a threefold meaning in Scripture—the literal or natural, the moral, and the mystical or spiritual. Corresponding to the threefold meaning were three levels of interpretation—the literal explaining the simple, obvious import of the passage, the moral relating it to practical conduct, and the mystical which drew out its latent relevance to Christ, his kingdom, and the mysteries of the faith. It is true that he took pains to elucidate the literal meaning; but it was "the moral and the mystical or divine wisdom" which really interested him. These were for him the two eyes wherewith Christ was seen, the two kinds of nutriment by which the inner life was sustained. His motive for preferring them was mainly that they assisted him to appreciate the relation of the Old to the New Testaments, and also to explain away any context which might seem unworthy of the Godhead or discreditable to the saints of Israel or the new law.

A brief reference to Augustine must conclude this all too rapid review. His whole literary achievement, as theologian, preacher, and polemist, was in effect a vast effort of biblical analysis and exposition. Harnack was stating the plain truth when he remarked that, if the Bible has occupied a very special position in the Western Church since the early fifth century, this is entirely due to him. It is all the more disappointing to observe that as an exegete he stands visibly below Jerome. His success— it was so impressive as to make him the greatest Christian thinker in the West—lay rather in apprehending and assimilating the deeper message of the Bible, or of such a biblical writer as St Paul, than in expounding individual passages. It is true that he had admirable exegetical principles; they are set out most conveniently in his *De doctrina christiana*, which he wrote between 396 and 426. He who would read the Bible correctly must be skilled in Greek and Hebrew, and ought to be well grounded in history, science, local customs and institutions, and so on. He should strive to bring out the true sense of each text faithfully, explaining the Bible as far as possible by the Bible, and resorting to allegory to smooth over inconsistencies, anthropomorphisms, apparent errors, and other such difficulties. In his own practice Augustine sometimes adheres to these principles, but all too often he throws them overboard. As a result partly of his controversial ardour, partly of his zeal for edification, and partly of the subtlety and fertility of his own imagination, he found the allurements of allegory and of fantastic mystical elucidations irresistible; and he revealed a curiously uncritical strain in the partiality he showed for what he regarded as the divinely inspired Septuagint. He was also responsible for a theory of the plurality of senses which would have ruined all sound, objective exegesis if it had prevailed. According to this, the reader is entitled to extract any meaning that occurs to him out of any passage, provided it is edifying and agreeable with other passages of Scripture, quite irrespective of whether the author intended it or not; and in so doing he can rest assured that the Holy Spirit foresaw and willed this interpretation.

What judgement are we to pass on the effort of the Latin Fathers to wrest from Holy Scripture its saving message? Looking back it is easy, all too easy for modern people with the intellectual development of the past three centuries behind them, to lay a finger on its obvious weaknesses and deficiencies. The scientific equipment of these Latin exegetes, it goes without saying, was woefully inadequate, but that is not our principal criticism. Much more serious and far-reaching were certain other features of their approach to the Bible at which we have glanced in passing. First, they were hampered by an altogether too narrow, too mechanical conception of inspiration; and they drew from it the fatal corollary of the absolute inerrancy of Scripture in all its parts. Secondly, while an entirely sound instinct made them perceive the organic connection between the revelations of the old and the new dispensations, they soon lost touch with the simpler and more reliable typological insights of the apostolic age and were intoxicated by the axiom that every minutest detail of the Old Testament should be read as prefigurative of Christ and his new order. Linked with this was what was perhaps the greatest gap in their understanding of the Bible—their failure to appreciate the significance of history, in particular its significance as the arena of God's progressive revelation. The net result was that, instead of frankly accepting the fact that the divine message was conveyed in earthen vessels and that God's activity and purpose can be discerned in events sometimes apparently trivial, they felt entitled, even obliged, to find the chief significance of much of the Bible in allegories and spiritual or mystical interpretations which were at best ingenious readings back into it of accepted Christian ideas and at worst entirely subjective fancies.

At the same time we are bound to recognize that, however defective their premises and however questionable much of their detailed exegesis, the broad outline of theological dogma which the Latin Fathers, along with their Greek coadjutors, constructed with the help of Scripture was, by and large, faithful to its essential message. This may sound paradoxical after the damaging criticisms we have passed, but the explanation is really quite simple. The fact is that, although it naturally sought confirmation of its dogmas in the Bible, the Church had not in the first instance found them there. It had received them first of all from its own living tradition dating back continuously to the apostles, and in reading the scriptures it was guided and kept on the right lines by that tradition. The great dogmas were of course present, explicitly or implicitly, in Scripture, which in its New Testament portion can be regarded as the codification of the tradition, but well before the New Testament was admitted as canonical they, or at any rate those fundamental beliefs which were to be formulated as dogmas, were being handed down to Christians in the Church's rule of faith, its catechetical system, its day-to-day life and worship. It is as a matter of fact noticeable that, when they are discussing strictly theological issues with a view to stating doctrine, Fathers like Hippolytus and Hilary and Augustine (to give but three examples) tend to adopt much more straightforward, rigorous methods of exegesis than when edification or ascetical instruction is their aim.

The Latin Fathers, as we admitted at the outset, rarely equalled the Greeks in range, originality, or brilliance, but within their limits they made a contribution of lasting value. When we study, for example, the long and often acrimonious arguments of Tertullian with the Marcionites or with Praxeas, we feel disposed to quarrel with him over and over again in his use of texts, but very few of us could doubt that the positions for which he was contending were essentially the Christian, biblical ones. We are conscious of exactly the same exegetical exaspera-tion combined with the same agreement of theological principle when we re-read the debates of Augustine (to take another instance at random) with contemporary Arians on the one hand and with the Donatists on the other. Again, Pelagius was in many respects (perhaps most respects) a sounder biblical scholar than Augustine, and the latter's reading of the Genesis story, not to mention his text of Romans 5, would find few defenders to-day; but most of us would probably agree that his doctrine of original sin, for all its darkness and exaggeration, more faithfully mirrors the scriptural view of man than does the optimism of his rival, If I may take another and final point, historians of dogma have often drawn attention to the charac-teristic emphases of Western theology which distinguish it from Eastern. In Trinitarian doctrine, for example, the West was always clearer about the divine unity than the nature of the personal distinctions, and we recall Augustine's embarrassment at the formula *tres personae*; and in Christology it is striking that all the great controversies took place in the East, the West being content with a common-sense doctrine which never doubted the oneness of the person of the God-man or the reality of each of his two natures. It is not far-fetched, as it seems to me, to find the explanation of these and other similar phenomena in the distinctively Western approach to the Bible. With their prefer-ence for Scripture to metaphysical speculation, and with their firm grasp of the rule of faith or creed and their determination to read Scripture in the light of it (a very typical example is Leo's rebuke to Eutyches in the first chapter of his Tome), it was natural that the Latin Fathers should express their faith in doctrinal formulations which may have lacked subtlety and profundity, but which held in tension the data of the biblical revelation.

The Bible in the Middle Ages

BERYL SMALLEY

An historian invited to speak to theologians will feel flattered and would normally also feel happily irresponsible. He cannot and should not take part in theological controversies. In this case, however, I shall be telling the pre-history of a modern controversy in which, as a member of Congregation at Oxford, I voted in public twice—the secularization of the Regius Professorship of Hebrew. So much for detachment!

The whole "middle age" is too long a period to cover in one lecture. I shall therefore concentrate on St Thomas Aquinas and his successors: the late thirteenth and fourteenth centuries saw the posing of a question which is still actual in biblical exegesis. The earlier middle ages may be called an age of innocence from this point of view. Biblical commentators continued the Latin patristic tradition already described to you. The spiritual interpretation according to the three spiritual senses (allegorical, moral, anagogical) appealed to them, as it had appealed to St Gregory the Great, as an answer to their special problems. They held the literal sense to be true and basic, but wrote of it in many contexts as though it were inferior to the spiritual; it was a necessary exegetical chore. They expressed their attitude in such phrases as *superficies litterae* (contrasted with a deep spiritual meaning) or the "fleshly sense" (the flesh imprisons or veils the spirit). The approach made for ambivalence and confusion. It set the commentator two problems without providing him with a method for answering them.

The word "literal" had a double meaning. Did literal interpretation cover metaphor, imagery, and parable, or should their interpretation be included in the spiritual? It was tempting

57

to deny them a literal interpretation and pass straight to allegory instead of first explaining the expression in its literal context. Secondly, what value should be given to allegories, moralities, etc. as proof texts supporting the commentator's thesis? The dangers of a subjective use of the spiritual interpretation in a theological debate were glaring. No argument, it was clearly recognized, could be presented in the form of an allegorical or moral interpretation unless it were also found in the literal sense. This held in theology proper, but commentators had a border area to skirmish over when they discussed politico-religious questions, where there was no agreed court of appeal. Defenders of the Church in her conflicts with the State relied on a spiritual interpretation of God's creation of the sun and the moon; the sun as the greater light signifies the Church, and the lesser light, reflecting the rays of the sun, signifies the State; Noah's ark signifies the Church too, saving men from the tempest of the world. The habit of quoting such proof texts spread to lesser disputes internal to the Church. Secular clergy in the early twelfth century contested the right of religious to preach to the people, to take tithes, and to exercise priestly functions *qua* monks on the grounds that these duties and the revenues attached to their performance had no place in primitive monasticism and had been usurped in recent times. An anti-monastic pamphlet by Theobald of Etampes, a secular master teaching at Oxford, and a reply by an anonymous religious have just been published in full.[1] The secular uses a semi-historical argument: the tribe of Levi and no other enjoyed first fruits and tithes; the tribe of Levi signifies the priesthood, not monasticism; it follows that monks have no right to pose as successors of the tribe of Levi. The monk puts forward the story of Isaac as an answer. The story has an allegorical sense, which is universally recognized: Abraham's sacrifice of Isaac figures the sacrifice of Christ on the Cross. But scripture has a number of spiritual senses. Hence we may conclude that Esau, the elder

---

[1] R. Foreville and J. Leclercq, "Un débat sur le sacerdoce des moines au XIIe siècle", *Studia Anselmiana. Analectica monastica* 41, 1957, pp. 8–119.

brother who gave away his birthright, signifies the secular clergy; they have forfeited their privilege by neglect of their spiritual duties and greed for temporal gain. Jacob signifies the religious, who enter into their inheritance. Isaac signifies God the Father, who tests and blesses the religious in the person of Jacob. Rebecca signifies Holy Mother Church, preferring her favourite to her elder son. The anonymous monk's prelude to his argument puts the twelfth-century attitude to Bible punching with splendid clarity:

> As often as the faithful strive among themselves to discuss passages of Holy Scripture concerning the health of souls, it is needful, if the matter requires it, to investigate first of all histories (i.e. to find historical arguments); then they should delicately search through the holy books to see whether allegorical sacraments lie hidden therein.[1]

Our monk was on the right side in the controversy in that history has justified him: the religious did hold their ground against the seculars. But history was soon to condemn his type of scriptural argument. It would not have satisfied a scholastic.

The French Jesuit, Père de Lubac, has just published a challenging book in which he makes a warm, persuasive plea for the spiritual interpretation as practised in the middle ages.[2] He argues that it enabled the student of scripture to bridge any gap that might open between the Old and New Testaments. The student could read them together as one divine revelation by means of allegory; he could find Christian morals taught in both Testaments by means of moralities; the anagogical interpretation closed that other gap which opens between the New Testament and the Last Things. The spiritual interpretation arose from and in turn created a religious approach to the Bible. Its subsequent neglect led students into devious and unrewarding paths. Père de Lubac has proved conclusively that medieval exegetes up to the early thirteenth century, where his last volume stops, used the spiritual interpretation with profit;

[1] Ibid., p. 108.
[2] H. de Lubac, *Exégèse médiévale. Les quatre sens de l'Ecriture*, Paris, 1959.

I should add "and with even more pleasure"; it offered such wonderful scope for imagination and for sheer cleverness. My own view is that from the period of St Thomas onward the profit lessened though the pleasure often remained.

St Thomas made a new approach to Bible study both possible and desirable. Neither he nor his master St Albert specialized in biblical scholarship, but both took an interest in literal interpretation. St Thomas restated the theory of the four senses so as to combine the received teaching of the Fathers with the newly understood Aristotelian philosophy of causation. The literal sense covered the whole meaning of the inspired writer; hence it necessarily included metaphor, imagery, and parable. The spiritual senses were those intended by God, the first author of scripture, and derived from the events of sacred history itself. Christians could find a spiritual meaning in the record of events, as when they saw the sacrifice of Isaac as prefiguring the sacrifice of Calvary. But an exegete expounding according to the literal sense must consider the inspired writers' intentions and ask what they meant. The spiritual interpretation by definition was something over and above their intention, something that they could not possibly have grasped. It could not be adduced in argument; one could use it for edification, but not to prove a point. A mere restatement of the relationship between the senses would have helped medieval scholars. They had groped their way towards including metaphor, imagery, and parable in the literal sense in spite of the ambivalence in their patristic sources. Now they had clear reason to do so. That some confusion had persisted appears from St Thomas's commentary on Job. His repetitive stress on the fact that his explanation of poetic imagery in his text belongs to the literary sense as being part of the writer's intention would be pointless had he been flogging a dead horse. A concise and systematic scholar will not repeat himself unless he runs the risk of being misunderstood. St Thomas did more than restate; he showed that literal exposition could be exciting and deep. His commentary on Job brings out the philosophical content of the book instead of treating it as a lesson in patience or a collection of allegories and moralities. Did he in his discreet way mean to explode forever the old view of the literal sense as superficial and fleshly? Readers of his commentary could certainly deduce as much from this experiment in exegesis. A recent study of St Thomas's teaching on the four senses suggests that he aimed at returning to the "authentic typologism of the New Testament writings" as against later developments in the handling of the spiritual senses.[1] This strikes me as a good guess; we shall never really know.

The Thomist restatement offered a challenge and posed the most actual of modern problems. Is the Bible to be read as a collection of historical documents in their differing historical contexts? If we look for the writers' intentions we cannot evade this question. If the answer be, "yes", then more problems pose themselves. You know more about them than I do. If you say, "yes, but not *only* in that way . . .", you must explain what you mean by "only". And you must begin by facing that first and crucial question. In the "age of innocence", as I have called the early middle ages, the spiritual interpretation would take care of whatever the literal interpretation left to be desired from a Christian point of view. Now that its scope had been restricted, biblical scholars had to shoulder a new responsibility. In considering the sequel to the Thomist restatement one must ask first of all whether it won general acceptance, secondly whether its challenge was taken up, and thirdly whether the ensuing debates resulted in any advance in late-medieval Bible study.

The Thomist theory of the relationship between the senses won acceptance quickly in some quarters, slowly in others.[2] It ended by being generally received. The papal chancery adopted the Thomist view that proof texts according to their spiritual interpretation were invalid as arguments in the conflict between Church and State. The function of theology in the drafting of papal bulls is no longer to "draw the lifegiving *spirit* from the

---

[1] M.-D. Mailhiot, "La pensée de S. Thomas sur le sens spirituel", *Revue Thomiste* 59, 1959, 613–63.
[2] B. Smalley, "Which William of Nottingham?", *Mediaeval and Renaissance Studies* 3, 1954, pp. 263–8.

letter that killeth", a reference to the older view, but to "draw out the lifegiving *sense* which is contained there (in Scripture) *very obscurely*". That is to say, the exegete concerns himself with deep matters; they need not refer to "allegories". The change in techniques of argument and in drafting occurs significantly in the pontificate of John XXII (1316–34), who canonized St Thomas.[1]

Some interesting essays in literal interpretation show that commentators under Thomist influence took a more positive view of their functions. The literal sense of the Old Testament had fascinated scholars from the early twelfth century onward. Some had studied Hebrew and Jewish traditions so as to throw fresh light on the original text and on its historical meaning.[2] Robert Grosseteste, Bishop of Lincoln, and a few disciples had learnt Greek in order to study the Septuagint, the Greek New Testament, and Byzantine commentaries.[3] All had been handicapped by the old concept of the *superficies litterae* and by its consequence that those who expounded "according to the letter" were second-class citizens. Now the master expounding his text in the literal sense could hold up his head, feeling that his task made demands on his whole energy and ability and that it had the utmost importance in the education of his pupils.

Ptolemy of Lucca, a pupil of St Thomas, wrote a literal exposition of the Hexaemeron or six days of creation. He aimed at bringing the data of natural science as understood in his day to bear on the account given in Genesis. A secular master of Paris, Henry of Ghent, by no means a thoroughgoing Thomist in his philosophy and theology, lectured on the same subject. Although he keeps to the literal interpretation, he regards his

[1] B. Smalley, "John Baconthorpe's Postill on St Matthew", ibid., 4, 1958, 142–3.
[2] B. Smalley, *The Study of the Bible in the Middle Ages*, 2nd ed., 1952; R. Loewe, "Herbert of Bosham's Commentary on Jerome's Hebrew Psalter", *Biblica* 34, 1953, pp. 44–7, 159–92, 275–98; "The Mediaeval Christian Hebraists of England", *Transactions of the Jewish Historical Society of England* 17, 1953, 225–49; "The Mediaeval Christian Hebraists of England. The Superscriptio Lincolniensis", *Hebrew Union College Annual* 28, 1957, 205–52.
[3] *Robert Grosseteste, Scholar and Bishop*, ed. D. A. Callus, Oxford, 1955.

course as a "ministry" and prays in his opening lecture that he
may suffer from no poverty of ideas, but rather rejoice in
"wonderful abundance".[1] His class may have felt that the
petition had its dangers. It was granted. Henry is drier and
more severely theological in his exposition than Ptolemy, but he
suffers from no poverty of ideas. He goes through his text
arranging a sort of exhibition of errors which have arisen
through the misconceptions of heathen philosophers and heretics
and criticizing interpretations of revered predecessors which
struck him as improbable, such as the view that the waters over
the firmament were set there to cool the stars and remained in
their place miraculously. He tried to determine the meaning
intended by the author of Genesis as distinct from the opinions
of his commentators. An anonymous commentator on St
Matthew surpassed even Henry in "wonderful abundance". His
book survives in a fragment covering Matt. 9. 18—10. 16. It
fills 465 leaves in the manuscript! We have no clue to his
identity. The manuscript, now in the Vatican Library, is
fourteenth-century and may have been written at Avignon, in
which case the commentator may have been lecturing at the
studium attached to the papal curia.[2] The Gospels of course were
always expounded in the literal sense, but commentators would
often use a moral and anagogical interpretation as well. This one
restricts himself mainly to the literal sense. He achieves his abundance by expounding a conflation of the gospel stories and by
making a vast compilation of excerpts from earlier commentaries. Numerous quotations from St Thomas point to the
source of his inspiration. What strikes me as interesting and
original is his attempt to fill in the psychological and human
background of his text. In default of new material it was all he
could do if he took the literal interpretation seriously. On

[1] B. Smalley, "A commentary on the Hexaemeron by Henry of Ghent",
Recherches de théologie ancienne et médiévale 20, 1953, 60–101.
[2] MS Rome, Bibl. Apost. Vat. Borgh. lat. 32, foll. 1–465v. See A. Maier,
"Codices Burghesiani", *Studi e testi* 170, 1952, p. 33. The hand suggests
Avignon to an expert on palaeography whom I consulted. A reference
backward, *ut supra dicebatur* (fol. 4v) leads one to suppose that the commentary on earlier chapters actually existed.

Matt. 9. 18 he explains why a father feels special affection for an only daughter (the reasons suggested are practical rather than sentimental); thus the father's joy at his daughter's recovery is brought home to the audience. On 9.20 he recalls the parallel in St Luke where we read that the suffering woman had spent all her substance on doctor's bills without being cured. This leads to remarks on the ways of doctors with their patients which are still topical. He discusses at length the meaning of *fimbria*.[1] Above all, he hopes to draw out the moral and religious teaching of the gospel in its literal sense.

Remigio of Florence, another pupil of St Thomas, set himself a harder task. He lectured on the Canticle with the aim of applying his master's teaching to this book of all books.[2] What was the literal meaning of Solomon's love song? It was currently explained as referring to Christ and the Church or to Christ and the faithful soul or to the Virgin. The only alternative that a medieval Christian exegete could find was the Jewish interpretation: God speaks to his chosen people. It would have been inconceivable then, as it still is to some readers, to see its origin in secular love songs. Remigio makes the tentative suggestion that Solomon when he composed the Canticle had in mind his love for Pharaoh's daughter, his dark but beautiful bride. She apologizes for her complexion because her brothers have made her work in the fields or vineyards at harvest time. Remigio glimpses the pastoral character of the songs. He includes the metaphors in the literal sense, but comes to the conclusion that in this case the spiritual senses belong to Solomon's intention; he used the language of secular songs, and thought of his own human feelings, but he wished to convey spiritual senses by these means. The spiritual senses, therefore, are part of the literal sense in its wider meaning, because they were consciously intended by the author. Remigio has faced his problem squarely.

An idea has come to stay when it gets into a textbook: the

[1] Foll. 9–10v, 25v, 28v.
[2] H. Riedlinger, "Die Makellosigkeit der Kirche in den lateinischen Hoheliedkommentaren des Mittelalters", *Beiträge zur Geschichte der Philosophie und Theologie des Mittelalters* 38, iii, 1958, pp. 336–40.

museum-like quality of textbooks is a constant source of wonder to modern teachers. An enterprising French Franciscan professor called Pierre Auriol undertook to compile a manual on the literal sense of the biblical books. His *Compendium litteralis sensus totius sacrae scripturae*, finished in 1319, had a great success; it seems to have been hailed as a kind of fourteenth-century Pfeiffer. Auriol grappled with the problem of classifying the sacred books as a prelude to digesting them. He chose literary type as his criterion: law, history, prophecy, ethics, song, debate, epistle, and so on. He had committed himself in advance to deciding on the literal sense of the Canticle and the Psalter, to mention two of the most difficult books. Did they contain prophecies of Christ in their literal sense? What words had Solomon or the psalmist intended to refer to Israel in an Old Testament context and what to the new dispensation? What, in fact, should go into the *Compendium litteralis sensus*? Auriol summarizes the Canticle in a purely Old Testament context as referring to the marriage between God and Israel. He also restricts the number of Christological psalms. He allows a Christological character to psalms which have *intellectus* or *titulus* in their titles and to no others. Some of Auriol's contemporaries may have been as surprised at his very arbitrary principle of selection as you are. The interesting point is that he felt some principle of choice to be necessary and would not interpret all psalms as prophecies of Christ.

Meanwhile an English Dominican called Nicholas Trevet was preparing literal commentaries and learning Hebrew for the purpose. Pope John XXII encouraged him; the whole order of Friars Preacher was instructed at a general chapter to help him in his work.[1] Trevet too rejected a wholesale Christological interpretation of the Psalter. It should be noted that early fourteenth-century scholars bracketed Trevet with his more famous contemporary, the Franciscan Nicholas of Lyre. They were quoted together by the type of lecturer who likes to offer

[1] A. B. Emden, *A Biographical Register of the University of Oxford to A.D. 1500*, 3, 1959, pp. 1902–4.

his pupils the best modern authors, while unable to contribute specialist data of his own. Lyre gave his whole attention to Bible studies. Like Trevet he had encouragement from the highest quarters. He expounded the whole Bible well before his death in 1349. His *Postilla litteralis* became a classic.[1]

Lyre drank a heady draught of Hebrew scholarship and proceeded, thus fortified, to discriminate between the literal and spiritual senses of Old Testament prophecy. He was neither rash nor self-assertive. Where he had sound guidance, as on the book of Job, he contented himself with following a medieval predecessor. He accepts St Thomas' views for the most part, correcting him on minor points; Lyre's knowledge of Hebrew enabled him to supply defects in St Thomas' commentary. The exposition of the Canticle and the Psalter threw him on his own resources. Here he opposed the two traditions of interpretation, Jewish and Christian. He tried to be fair to the Jews. They interpreted the Canticle as referring to the marriage between God and Israel; the Christians saw it as a prophecy of the marriage between Christ and his Church. Both sides according to Lyre ran into *inconvenientia*: the text would seem to favour now one and now the other interpretation. He decided to share out the Canticle between them. The Jews did rather well out of it. They got chapters 1 to 6 and the Christians only chapters 7 and 8.[2] His Psalter-commentary is a manifesto. He laid down the following principles of distinction: psalms may be classed as Christological in their literal sense (i) if they are so quoted in the New Testament, (ii) if the rabbis of old (*antiqui iudaei*) interpreted them as messianic; Lyre knew that Rashi had refused the traditional messianic sense to certain psalms because Christians had relied on them in their anti-Jewish polemic, (iii) if the actual words of the prophecy seemed to lend themselves better to a New than to an Old Testament context. These three principles of distinction led Lyre to interpret the majority of psalms in relation to

[1] *Histoire littéraire de la France* 36, 1927, pp. 355–400. Lyre's *Postilla* was published in many editions along with the *Glossa ordinaria* and the *Additiones* of Paul of Burgos. I use the edition made at Lyons, 1588–90.

[2] H. Riedlinger, op. cit., pp. 371–3.

Old Testament history. He admitted some twenty-six as Christological in their literal sense. One case struck him as doubtful; in another he found a mixture of New and Old Testament references. A few psalms he thought would apply equally well to God-fearing men at any time.

The scene had been set for a fundamental discussion. Exegetes had broached an essential question in their handling of the Old Testament at least. With primitive techniques and the merest inkling of historical perspective they had anticipated what, I suppose, is the main subject of this lecture course. They had seen something that the spiritual interpretation had tended to conceal: the Jewish background of the Old Testament demanded rethinking of method. It looked as though later medieval trends of thought would favour biblical scholarship. A "back-to-the-Bible" movement began at both Oxford and Paris. Though John Wyclif ended as a heretic, while Jean Gerson remained orthodox, they agreed in recalling their colleagues from modern to patristic authors and in focusing attention on the Bible. Would the Thomist teaching on the senses combine with scholarship of Lyre's type within the framework of late-medieval biblicism? *Funiculus triplex difficile rumpitur.* It did not happen. The three strands never mingled.

Thomism as a system of thought went out of fashion in the fourteenth century to be replaced by scepticism and fideism. Neither was propitious to biblical scholarship. A sharply critical sense deriving from the new logic made it unsafe to look too closely at the data of revelation. St Thomas' actual teaching on the senses remained standard; the eagerness and daring of the doctor and his disciples died. So did the study of biblical languages. Lyre was the last famous Hebraist of his century. Experience has shown that an academic discipline may languish if left to the initiative of individuals, as Hebrew was in medieval studies. Endowment of chairs is the best guarantee of continuity in teaching. The Council of Vienne of 1311–12 ordered the setting up of chairs for the study of Greek and oriental languages in the leading *studia* of Latin Christendom and arranged for their endowment from local ecclesiastical revenues. Although the movers of the decree had in mind primarily mission work among the heathen, biblical studies would clearly have benefited. The decree remained a dead letter.[1] Presumably qualified teachers were too scarce and nobody took enough interest in the project to carry it through. Then the Oxford and Prague heresies of the turn of the fourteenth century put a new premium on safety and caution. They also, together with the Great Schism and the Conciliar movement, directed the energies of scholars into other channels. Pressing questions demanded action and propaganda.

Meanwhile the spiritual interpretation continued to flourish. Excluded from serious scholastic argument, it still had a part to play in homiletics. Tradition and practical need made it indispensable to teachers and preachers, who had to instruct their audiences in faith and morals. The chair and the pulpit were two organs for the same type of instruction; the lecturer on scripture was training his pupils to preach. The teaching of scripture was wedded to homiletics. We know only too well nowadays the dangers that come from over-specialization. The dilemma remains: some specialization is necessary before a subject can develop. Theologians of the late twelfth and thirteenth centuries had taken a step towards specialization when they separated doctrinal theology from the teaching of scripture. Lectures on the *Sentences* of Peter Lombard and disputations relieved the lecturer on scripture of a heavy burden. Conservatives bewailed the separation, but it brought progress in both branches of theology. The schoolmen of the later middle ages, however, would carry specialization no further. They did not consider separating exegesis from pastoral theology.

A certain mental dishonesty and frivolity resulted from the continued use of allegories and moralities in exegesis. Dishonesty because they were no longer regarded as deep sacraments as they had been in the pre-scholastic period, frivolity because they

---

[1] A. G. Little, *Studies in English Franciscan History*, Manchester, 1917, pp. 215–18; R. Weiss, "England and the Decree of the Council of Vienne," *Bibliothèque d'Humanisme et de Renaissance* 14, 1952, pp. 1–9.

had worn so threadbare. To-day, when the spiritual senses have the freshness of a new discovery, it is difficult to imagine how time had staled them. Every text of the Bible which lent itself to the process had been allegorized and moralized with varying shades of ingenuity. Homilists turned to profane texts and stories for a change. They would moralize whatever came their way. They even invented tales on their own account as subjects for the spiritual interpretation. Here is an example from a lecture course on the Epistle to Titus, given at Paris in the year 1363. The lecturer, Jean de Hesdin, is better known for his brush with Petrarch than as a commentator, but he was popular in the latter capacity in the fourteenth and fifteenth centuries. He has to consider the virtues required of a good bishop as listed in the Epistle. The bishop must be *just*:

> Since we now have justice on hand, we shall say something on the subject. . . . First we must see for our solace (*causa solationis*) how the ancients depicted the image of justice, and bring it to bear on right conduct for our instruction.

Hesdin then collects from his medieval and ancient sources a composite picture of justice personified, with various attributes, each of which he will proceed to moralize.[1] *Causa solationis* perhaps implies "now for some light relief"! He makes no pretence of thinking that his morality has any deeper significance. The professor is simply admitting that the Apostle's teaching sounds rather trite and dull as it stands; he puts on twirls and flourishes, employing a mechanical device to keep his hearers quiet while he tells them to be good. The extension of spiritual interpretation from the Bible to profane texts of recent invention must have lowered it in men's eyes; or else they possessed a pigeon-hole mentality to a degree uncommon even among teachers. I have used the metaphor of a wedding between scholarship and homiletics; the latter in fourteenth-

[1] B. Smalley, "Jean de Hesdin O. Hosp. S. Ioh.", *Recherches de théologie ancienne et médiévale* 28, 1962, pp. 328–9. On moralization of invented stories and "pictures" see J. T. Welter, *L'exemplum dans la littérature religieuse et didactique du Moyen Age*, Paris, Toulouse, 1927; B. Smalley, *English Friars and Antiquity in the Early Fourteenth Century*, Oxford, 1960.

century dress reminds me of a silly, gay young wife who never leaves her husband alone.

We know too little of fifteenth-century exegesis to judge it. Erasmus has done so for us. He believed himself to be doing something new when he corrected the Vulgate text from his knowledge of Greek and his collation of early manuscripts, and when he cleaned off the medieval glosses. Contemporary theologians put up a furious resistance, ignorant, it seems, of the fact that Erasmus was carrying on a tradition of scholarship which had been respectable enough in the early fourteenth century. The presumption until further research has been done is that Lyre's type of scholarship did not revive. A recent monograph on a Psalter-commentary of the late fifteenth century bears out this impression.[1] The Austin friar, Jaime Perez, taught at Valencia and died as suffragan bishop of the diocese in 1490. He wrote his Psalter-commentary for the instruction of the cathedral clergy 1460–5. Perez would have agreed with Père de Lubac in praise of the spiritual interpretation. He wanted to return to the Fathers, and to St Augustine especially. The spiritual interpretation pleased him for the same reason: it made a *heilsgeschichtlich* view of scripture possible. The allegorical interpretation seemed to Perez to be called for in a world which suffered from loss of faith. He would combat neo-paganism and indifference by teaching the Christian faith in a scriptural framework as had been done in earlier periods. At the same time Perez could not simply pass over the work of St Thomas and of Lyre. He accepted the Thomist view of the relations between the senses and the fruits of Lyre's studies on the Hebrew sources. But he refused to follow Lyre in allowing a Christological sense in the literal exposition to selected psalms and not to the whole Psalter. Lyre, he thought, had been blasphemously wrong. The whole Psalter must bear a Christological interpretation according to the literal sense: "David was no less a prophet in *this* psalm than in others!", he cries repeatedly. Perez wanted

[1] W. Werbeck, "Jacobus Perez von Valencia. Untersuchungen zu seinem Psalmenkommentar", *Beiträge zur historischen Theologie* 28, 1959.

to recreate the image of his psalmist as a patristic seer. It is seldom feasible to copy one's model exactly. The Latin Fathers had cared little, if at all, for the problem that fascinated Lyre. To put it crudely: just what was the psalmist aiming at when he made his prophecies? The question could hardly be evaded, once asked. Perez answered it by manipulating his divergent traditions in a way that falsified them all. He did follow Lyre in referring many psalms to their Old Testament background in their literal sense. The psalmist had seen this clearly. But the psalmist also had a pervasive foreknowledge of Christian history, though he apprehended it more dimly. Hence he *intended* to prophesy of Christ and his Church and to teach Christian morals in each psalm, sometimes directly and sometimes under Old Testament figures. The spiritual senses were therefore subsumed in the literal sense, because the psalmist *meant* them to be all present together. Perez has added something foreign to his patristic authors while trying to wriggle out of the distinctions made by his medieval forerunners. He was a well-meaning cheat. True, Remigio of Florence had taken the same line in his commentary on the Canticle; Perez adopts it in his own commentary on this book,[1] as well as in his Psalter-commentary. To apply the method of including the spiritual in the literal sense to the Psalter was a different matter. It meant going behind Lyre, Auriol, Trevet, and earlier scholars. It meant throwing overboard the fruits of some hard, honest thinking.

An age of innocence will appeal to those who like what Croce calls "nostalgic history". Those who see history rather as a record of change will prefer to study the rise of new problems. St Thomas and some of his successors had begun to see the problem that still concerns you. The exegetes of the later middle ages turned away from it. I have led you up a blind alley. To explain why men pushed so far and then lost heart would take us outside the scope of this lecture course. Such reasons as might be suggested would anyway have to be guesses and these would be personal to the historian.

[1] H. Reidlinger, op. cit., 373–5.

The Bible in the Age of the Reformation

E. G. RUPP

ON almost any reckoning, the sixteenth century would have been a century of storm and violence. The invention of printing, the growth of great publishing houses, the development of an international book traffic made sure that at the heart of it there should be an ideological ferment, a battle of books. Through the printed word other men of other centuries joined in the debate, and historians have yet to evaluate the explosive material which came now to hand: apocalyptic writings like those of Joachim or the Spiritual Franciscans: mystic treatises like those of Hildegard of Bingen, Suso, Tauler: philosophic speculations like the works of Cusanus or the Hermetic writings: the new editions of the Greek and Latin classics: the Fathers of East and West. It is arguable that the most important single sixteenth-century voice came from the past—that of St Augustine. There can be no doubt at all what was the most influential book; it was the Bible. The other explosive literature stood in relation to it as nuclear weapons to the Great Bomb itself, and like it, the Bible had drastic effect on short and long term ecclesiastical strategy.

That this was so is due in the first place to humanism, and especially to those scholars north of the Alps who combined zeal for "good" and "sacred" letters. For in an important respect the Bible was just another ancient book. Its investigation has to be seen against the reappraisal of a whole literature recaptured from the past. The use of allegory, for example, was common to the interpretation of the Bible, of the Homeric writings, and of the Hebrew Cabbala. Above all, the great debate about the vernacular Bible was part of a general crisis

73

about translation, and how significant was this attempt to turn the thought and word-world of one age into that of another has been profoundly suggested recently by Mr H. A. Mason in his brilliant and provoking study of Humanism and Poetry.[1]

There was first the return to the sacred languages of Greek, Hebrew, and a renovated Latin. But this was early seen to have implications for the interpretation of the Bible. Dr Schwarz has shown how the new critical method raised the question whether orthodoxy must not now be subservient to the exact philological exegesis of the sacred text.[2] Laurentius Valla, the edition of whose *Notes on the New Testament* by Erasmus (published by Badius in 1505) was an important landmark, had no doubt about it.

> There are those who believe that theology is not subservient to the rules of grammar. But I say that theology must observe the usage of the spoken and especially of the written language.[3]

John Reuchlin insisted that the appeal must be to the original languages:

> I would have you know that nobody of the Latin people has been able to give an exact explanation of the Old Testament without having first had knowledge of the language in which it was written.

The sacred languages: the oldest manuscripts, the best text. Antonio Lebrixa, the boldest and most brilliant of the scholars of the Alcalá put it thus:

> Every time we are faced with variant readings in the New Testament, let us go to the Greek MSS: every time there are disagreements between the different Latin and Greek MSS of the Old Testament, let us seek the rule of truth in the Hebrew source.[4]

The first monuments of the critical method came from Catholic humanism: the Complutensian Polyglot and the New Testament of Erasmus. The Polyglot was the product of a team

---

[1] H. A. Mason, *Humanism and Poetry in the Early Tudor Period*, 1959, pp. 23ff.
[2] W. Schwarz, *Principles of Biblical Translation*, 1955.
[3] Schwarz, p. 133. [4] Ibid, p. 78.

of Spanish scholars led by the Cardinal Ximenes. It was in many respects superior to the version of Erasmus, in its beautiful type for example and in its care for detail. But it dared not call in question the authority of the Vulgate, merely establishing a good text and setting a new Greek text by its side. It was a great pity that it was not published at once, but the Alcalá team proved to be as accident-prone as an England cricket eleven, so that though finished in 1514 it was not published until 1522.[1] By that time all the Top People had been reading Erasmus for some years! He had taken to heart the lessons of Valla's *Notes* and though he disliked Hebrew and indeed had no taste for the Old Testament generally, he became a Greek enthusiast, so that his New Testament was designed to give priority to a better Greek text. This was published by Frobenius in 1516 and to it he added a new Latin version. His scholarship was always hasty and slapdash and though he used the best and oldest manu- scripts he could get, they were not perhaps as good as he thought they were. And when he found Greek verses missing from his text of the Apocalypse he wrote them himself in Greek from the Latin. To the critical venturesomeness both of the Spaniards and of Erasmus there were limits. The Complutensians did not dare to question the notorious "comma Johanneum" of the Three Heavenly Witnesses. Erasmus did, and he boldly omitted it from the first three versions of his New Testament, and explained why he had done so. Then, with one of those gestures which his friends diagnosed as loyal faith, his enemies as failure of nerve, he reinserted it "to take away the excuse of calumny" —even though he had in the meantime discovered the passage to be missing from the Codex Vaticanus.

To some extent the spiritualism of the northern humanists blurred their critical approach. Most of them dabbled in the revived Platonism, like Reuchlin who found esoteric divine messages in the vowel points of the Bible and the Cabbala. Even John Colet, Le Fèvre, and Erasmus, for all their biblicism thought of the relation of text and meaning on the analogy of

[1] M. Bataillon, *Érasme et L'Espagne*, pp. 32ff.

body–soul and conceived it along one-sidedly spiritualistic lines. But let us not underestimate the daring of Erasmus. The Englishman Edward Lee, the Fleming Latomus, the Spaniard Zuñiga began an attack on Erasmus which never let up during his life and brought his works to the Index after his death. Moreover, Erasmus' new Latin version had all the fresh attraction that a Moffatt or J. B. Phillips has had for undergraduate minds. The young men at Cambridge vied in getting hold of it. Thomas Bilney says that "allured rather by the Latin than the Word of God I bought it". For Bilney it was a costly purchase: for the reading of it converted him and brought him to the fire. Again, Erasmus appended to his version an introductory essay which was a genuine manifesto. He recalled men from the arid subtleties of late scholasticism to the pages of the Gospels, to the simple "philosophy of Christ" and to the letters of St Paul. He boldly championed the cause of the open Bible in a famous and beautiful passage:

> Would that they might be translated into all the languages of all Christian people, that they might be read and known not merely by the Scotch and the Irish but by the Turks and Saracens. I wish that the husbandman might sing parts of them at the plough: that the weaver may warble them at his shuttle: that the traveller may with their narratives beguile the weariness of the way.[1]

Away in the West of England the words struck fire in the imagination of a young priest, William Tyndale who echoed them in controversy:

> If God spare my life ere many years I will cause a boy that driveth the plough to know more of the Scripture than thou dost.[2]

Finally, the Erasmus version had notes and glosses. Some such technical comments were needed in an age without philological commentaries. But other notes were far from academic, and were as biting as anything written by later Reformers. So he comments on 1 Cor. 14. 19 on worship in an unknown tongue:

---

[1] Erasmus, *Works*, ed. Holborn, I, 142, 202ff.
[2] J. F. Mozley, *William Tyndale*, 1937, p. 34.

There is so much of this in England that the monks attend to nothing else. A set of creatures who ought to be lamenting their sins, fancy that they can please God by gargling in their throats.

The Paraphrases of Erasmus which were turned into English and chained in churches by order of Edward VI must in their simple retelling have brought the gospel stories home afresh. Thus, of the raising of Jairus' daughter:

> Such as are in a deep sleep cannot many times be awakened, although men call them oftentimes with a loud voice, and pinch them never so much: and when they be called up yet do they not by and by awake, but being half awake and drowsy, gape, stretch their arms, nod their heads, that many times the chin striketh the breast: and if a man call not still upon them, they fall asleep again. But this dead maiden arose forthwith and walked at the voice of Jesus.

Erasmus lived to see and ridicule a new kind of hypocrite, one who ostentatiously carried the new version of the Bible around with him. So in the colloquy between Cannius and Polyphemus:

> Cannius: How provest thou that thou lovest the Gospel?
> Polyphemus: There was a certain gray friar which never ceased to babble and rail against the New Testament of Erasmus. . . . I laid this New Testament on his pate as hard as I could drive, and I made three bumps on his head, as big as three eggs in the Name of the Father and of the Son and of the Holy Ghost.
> Cannius: Truly this is, as they say, to defend the Gospel with the Gospel.[1]

Muscular Christianity with a vengeance!

Martin Luther's German Bible emerged at an appropriate moment in the great drama in which he became involved. From the beginning his own spiritual inquiries had been closely linked with biblical study, and notably into the meaning of the "Righteousness of God". As professor of biblical theology he had lectured for years on the text of the Scriptures: using at first the old threefold, fourfold hermeneutic, then seeking the one authentic sense: using, too, the new humanist tools as they

[1] Vocht, *The Earliest English Translation of Erasmus' Colloquies*, 1928, p. 24.

came along, Le Fèvre's beautiful edition of the Psalms (1513) and the new editions of Erasmus. By 1517 he had made Wittenberg a centre of renovated theological studies and could write:

> Our theology and that of St Augustine are going ahead. Nobody can hope for an audience unless he professes this theology: i.e. the Bible or St Augustine or some doctor of real authority in the Church.

The opening of the Church struggle in October 1517 raised new problems for which he sought an answer in the Bible and Ernst Bizer has recently shown how the interview with Cajetan in 1518 marks a stage in his evaluation of the relation of Scripture and the sacraments.[1] After the great Leipzig Disputation of 1519 Luther turned to examine doctrines of authority which till now he had not doubted and soon he set forth the paramount authority of Scripture over Pope and councils in his great treatises of 1520. The turning point at the Diet of Worms was his refusal to recant unless convinced by evident reason and the Word of God, and in the semi-private interviews which followed he would not budge from this position. Then, alone, thrown back on himself in the friendly prison of the Wartburg, high up in the Thuringian forest "in the region of the birds", he turned to translate the New Testament.

He never believed that good translations could come from one man and he enlisted a powerful team with better technical equipment than his own. But his helpers soon realized that he was the great master.

Though humility in the presence of the great had not been a noticeable characteristic of Martin Luther, he really did sit down like a little child with meekness and reverence before the Word of God. As his tracts had already shown, the German language was fluently alive in his mind which teemed with a Shakespearean or Miltonic richness. He thought much about his German language and about the problems of translation and has left an account of his principles in his two books against

---

[1] E. Bizer, *Fides ex auditu*, 1958.

Emser and in his open letter about translation.[1] As a careful workman he compares more than favourably with Erasmus:

> Sometimes for three or four weeks we have sought and asked for a single word and sometimes we have not found it even then. In working at the book of Job, Master Phillip, Aurogallus and I could sometimes scarcely finish three lines in four days.

He got Spalatin to borrow the court jewels so that he might see with his own eyes the colours of the precious stones mentioned in Revelation and he went down to the slaughter house to watch how animals were killed. The racy, proverbial speech which was his peasant inheritance he marvellously welded into the precise language of the polite court society in which his friend Spalatin moved. Perhaps the best tribute to him comes from Eastern Germany to-day where the authorities have arranged an exhibition in the Wartburg showing Luther's poetic gifts, his flair for the right word, and if Luther the great philologist is not the whole or the most important Luther, it is part of the truth to be remembered here.

In his own day his opponents paid him the compliment of using his work even when they denounced it. Jerome Emser complained shrilly that he had found over 1,400 mistranslations, but when his own version appeared it was plain that he had lifted Luther wholesale. Thomas Müntzer and the radicals denounced the biblicism of the new Scribes of Wittenberg, with their "Bible, bibble, babble", but they filled their own polemic with scriptural citations in the main derived from him. Luther called such his "ungrateful pupils", but he had some thankful ones too, beginning with William Tyndale, and other Bibles in other lands were indirectly his debtors. All his life long he laboured to amend his Bible, and Professor Bainton has pointed out that the last printed page on which he ever looked was a proof page of the latest revision. By the time he died in 1546 hundreds of thousands of copies had been printed, many of them finely illustrated, and Luther's Bible had struck swiftly and deeply into the spiritual life of the German people.

[1] *Works of Martin Luther* (Philadelphia), 8, pp. 275ff; 5, pp. 7ff.

In the great cities of South Germany and of Switzerland, humanists, reformation, and the Bible were closely associated. Of special interest are the lectures which the great layman of St Gall, Joachim Vadianus, gave in the beginning of 1523 on the Acts of the Apostles. It was for him a congenial theme. Like St Luke, Vadianus was a medical doctor: hardly at this time a "beloved physician" or at least it took him a long time to live down his behaviour during his first plague when he confined his attentions to writing helpful notes from a safe distance and an admirable leaflet on "What to do in time of plague". But he was also very much a don, a learned geographer who had a curiously modern habit of dragging his students out with him on expeditions—up Mount Pilatus, for example to look for a magic lake, and down into the bowels of a Polish salt mine. So that when he got his small audience (he lectured in Latin in a little town) to Acts 12 he paused and made a giant geographical excursus lasting many weeks. He seems to have believed that not only all St Gall was divided into three parts, but the whole earth, for the excursus was later published as a "description of the three parts of the habitable world". Then he settled down again at Acts 13, and those of us who had the missionary journeys of St Paul seared into our adolescent souls will find grim interest in the fact that Vadianus was probably the first to lecture on this theme, with maps, in the modern world. But it was not all academic fuss: Vadianus brought his hearers face to face with primitive Christianity, and if he converted none of his audience he may well have converted himself, for it was in these months that he crossed the invisible dividing line between what Belloc called "an ineffectual don" and a powerful Reformer.[1]

The Bible was at the heart of the Zürich Reformation. Huldrych Zwingli had been trained in humanism, after the School of Vadianus "atte" Vienna, and then became a devoted Erasmian. One of the treasures of the Zürich library is the copy of the Pauline Epistles which he transcribed with his own hands.

[1] W. Näf, *Vadianus and St Gall*, Vol. 2, 1957.

At some point not easy to date he turned from humanism to the Bible.

> When about seven or eight years ago I undertook to devote myself wholly to the Scriptures I was always prevented by philosophy. But eventually I came to the point where, led by the Word and Spirit of God I saw the need to set aside these things and learn the doctrine of God direct from his word. Then I began to ask God for light . . . and the Scriptures became clearer to me.

One way and another most of the turning points in the Zürich Reformation were concerned with the Bible. The first was when the new people's priest ascended the pulpit of the Gross Münster and, leaving the usual method, began to expound verse by verse the Gospel according to St Matthew—the beginning of a ministry of gospel and prophetic and expository preaching. The Evangelical Mandate of the Zürich Council, the first to go out from these cities, perhaps as early as 1520, ordered preachers to proclaim the Holy Gospels and the letters of the Holy Apostles, in line with the Spirit of God and of both Testaments of Holy Scripture. Then came the great Disputation of 29 January 1523, where the evangelical preachers sat with the Council in a solid block in the Gross Münster behind three open Bibles, in the Greek, Hebrew, and the Latin tongues. When John Faber, the Vicar General of the Bishop of Constance cried out in alarm at the way things were going, and said that a judge must be appointed for this disputation, Zwingli retorted, "The Spirit of God out of the Scriptures shall be the judge", and carried the great audience with him. He gathered round him a group of scholars, Leo Jud, Pellicanus, Bibliander, and out of their expositions of the Old Testament, the famous "prophesyings", there emerged the fine Zürich Bible. The last half of this decade saw an immense concentration on biblical theology: in Zürich, in Basel where Oecolampadius lectured on books of Old and New Testament to an audience which included several hundred citizens: in Strassburg where another learned company, Bucer, Capito, Hedio, Lambert of Avignon produced a series of Latin commentaries on the biblical books which found an enthusiastic public among the younger divines at distant Cambridge and at Oxford.

For these scholars the writings of the Fathers of West and East were of great importance, though in the main it was to them as expositors of Scripture that they looked. The Colloquy at Berne in 1528 was the great field day. To Berne the tribes came up, Capito, Bucer, Zwingli, Vadianus, bringing their sheaves. Their host, Haller, rummaged round for sacred texts but had to write some three weeks beforehand to say that he could not get hold of a Greek Old Testament though his bag included a Hebrew one and a Greek New Testament and some Hebrew grammar and some writings of the Fathers. The key note was struck in the noble opening thesis—"The Christian Church is born out of the Word of God, and in the same shall she abide, and not listen to the voice of strangers." And learned though the debate was, in Greek and Hebrew on occasion—it was ruled that all appeals to human authorities should be stricken from the record. The Bible, they said, the Bible alone was the authority for Protestants and one wonders how far the disputes with Anabaptists were responsible for this concentration. This group of learned Reformers, Zwingli, Oecolampadius and Bullinger, Bucer, Capito, Peter Martyr, Wolfgang Musculus were the founding fathers of reformed, as distinct from Lutheran Protestantism, resting on the authority of the Bible, but not neglectful of the "Old Fathers". John Calvin crowned this succession: his patristic learning was impressive (upwards of 4,000 citations from St Augustine)—but the main stress of his learning is seen in the massive series of biblical expositions on almost all the books of the Bible.

The Reformation brought a new hermeneutic in the train of a new critical method, and here we can only point to the seminal studies of Gerhard Ebeling for its discussion.[1] The Reformers themselves did not go closely into the differentia between the Word of God and the Bible. For them the canon was more like

[1] G. Ebeling, *Evangelienauslegung. Luthers Hermeneutik*, 1941 and art "Hermeneutik", *Religion in Geschichte und Gegenwart* (rev. ed.), 1959.

a ray of light with blurred edges than a box with sharp sides. So they could sometimes be surprising in their freedom, as for example Luther, Zwingli, Calvin who all on occasion disparaged the Apocalypse or Luther with his comparative judgement about the Epistle of James. If they all accepted some sort of kerygmatic norm, they tried to think against the background of the whole biblical testimony. It was not until Protestant orthodoxy became immersed in argument with the Jesuits that the question of inerrancy became important and there could emerge such statements as that of Quenstedt that:

> the holy canonical scriptures in their original text are the infallible truth and free from every error—there is no lie, deceit, no error even the slightest but every word is true . . . whether it pertains to doctrine, ethics, history, chronology, typography . . .[1]

The German Bible came under radical attack because it was a product of learning, of a teaching Church. Urbanus Rhegius says that Thomas Müntzer sought to discredit the Bible by teaching the peasants direct from nature. He probably refers to the interesting "gospel of all creatures" taught by some of the first Anabaptists and expounded in a homily on Mark 16. It claims that Jesus did not teach from books, except when he had to argue with the Scribes, but he spoke to common men in the idiom of natural things and of their daily occupations. The view is here put forward, perhaps derived from Raymond of Sabunde that God has given us two books, the one the Holy Scripture written in words, and the other the Book of Nature where all that is in holy writ is shown in deeds.[2] But the radical answer to the growing Lutheran objectivity was not this evanescent natural theology but an emphasis on the Inner Word and on the Holy Spirit. There was a great debate in the 1520s on the relation between the Outward and Inner Word. For the Reformers both concepts are important for their doctrine of the Bible.

[1] R. Preuss, *The Inspiration of Scripture*, 1955, p. 77.
[2] See E. G. Rupp, "Thomas Müntzer, Hans Huth and the 'Gospel of All Creatures' ", *Bulletin of John Rylands Library*, March 1961.

Luther developed the theme in his debate with Erasmus who had stressed (shades of 1516!) the difficulty and the obscurity of the Scriptures. But no, says Luther, Christ has opened them. "What solemn truth can the Scriptures hide now that the seals are broken, the stone rolled away from the door of the tomb?" He went on to distinguish between the external and the internal clarity of the Word. The external clarity is that of objective revelation itself, the *kerygma*, so that in his Torgau sermon Luther could speak of the Apostles' Creed as his "little Bible". This revelation is plain and clear—"who will maintain that the public fountain does not stand in the light, because some people in a back alley cannot see it when everybody in the market place sees it quite plainly?" And this is recorded in the Scriptures and announced in the preaching of the Gospel.[1] But no less important is the internal clarity of the Word, the Holy Spirit which, in a later phrase, speaks to our condition, by bringing home to each soul the meaning of the gospel, for me, and thereby giving believers an assurance of comfort and of joy.[2] There is a similar attempt to balance objectivity and subjectivity in Zwingli's masterly oration "On the Clarity and the Certainty of the Word of God". Wolfgang Musculus seeks to confute opponents with a curious image.

> Let them leave their looks of Great Elephants and begin to be simple lambs and let them enter into the rivers of Scripture in the fear of the Lord unto the bottom of which the lamb pierceth when the Elephant swimmeth above.[3]

He does not seem to have based his comment on very scientific observation.

Peter Martyr in "Exhortation to private Bible reading" expounds the internal clarity of the Word:

> For herein we hear not the wisdom of man, but have God himself speaking before us, to whom if we give ear we shall conceive singular joy, we shall chase away pensive cogitations, and be lightened with most sweet comfort: we shall be strengthened

[1] See R. Herrmann, *Von der Klarheit der Heiligen Schriften*, 1958.
[2] Østergaard-Nielsen, *Scriptura sacra et viva Vox*, 1957, pp. 114ff.
[3] W. Musculus, *Commonplaces* (Eng. Tr.), 1562, fol. 151.

beyond the condition of man: nothing shall be thought hard and shameful for us.[1]

Against the Catholic assertion that the Scriptures derive authority from the Church the Reformers stressed that its authority is in its own truth and majesty—it is "autopiston". This is the doctrine finely expounded by Calvin in the first Book of his Christian Institution. "They demand—how? This is all as though a man should ask how shall we learn to know light from darkness, white from black, or sweet from sour?" [2] Yet for Calvin too, this doctrine, as Werner Krusche [3] has shown, is bound up with his doctrine of the internal testimony of the Holy Spirit and in his teaching the two entities of Word and Spirit which Protestant controversy was putting asunder, are restored as one. The English Reformers stressed the same truth. When Stephen Gardiner railed at John Rogers —"Thou canst prove nothing by the Scriptures, the Scripture is dead, it needs a living expositor"—Rogers retorted, "No, the Scripture is alive!" Tyndale made the incomparable answer to Sir Thomas More.

> Who taught the eagles to spy out their prey? Even so the Children of God spy out their Father, and Christ's elect spy out their Lord and trace out the paths of his feet, and follow. Yea, and though he be upon the plain and liquid water which will receive no step, and yet there they find out his feet: his elect know him.

There was of course a weighty case against the open Bible. It did not go by default. It is to be read in the debate between Sir Thomas More and William Tyndale, between Luther and Emser and Cochlaeus, between William Fulke and Gregory Martin. In England the conservatives fought stubbornly with wooden arguments like those of Standish in 1540:

> The universal church of Christ did never approve scripture to be in the vulgar tongue, weighing the manifest inconveniences that have issued therefrom . . . the well must be covered, lest the younglings fall into it and be drowned.

[1] P. Martyr, *Commonplaces* (Eng. Tr.), 1583, fol. 44.
[2] J. Calvin, *Christian Institution*, Bk. 1, chs. 7, 8.
[3] W. Krusche, *Das Wirken des Heiligen Geistes nach Calvin*, 1957, pp. 184ff.

And nevertheless, the great chain reaction went on—William Tyndale, John Rogers, Miles Coverdale—the Great Bible—the Geneva Bible—The Bishops' Bible—the Douai Bible—the Authorized version. At first proscribed and contraband, read secretly by Anne Boleyn and her ladies of the Court, or fished out of its straw hiding place at night by the prentice William Maldon. When in 1543 the Bible was permitted in Scotland John Knox wrote an ironical flashback:

> Then might the Bible have been seen lying upon almost every gentleman's table . . . they would chop their familiars on the cheek with it and say—this has laid under my bed foot these ten years . . . others would glory "O how often have I stolen from my wife at midnight to read upon it."[1]

Very swiftly the Bible struck root among the laity. Urbanus Rhegius wrote to Erasmus in 1522:

> Recently I heard a matron who was able to discuss the relation between Law and Gospel in the Epistle to the Romans more learnedly than many of our doctors.[2]

Bishop Edward Foxe, newly come out of Germany, told Convocation in 1537:

> The lay people do know the Holy Scriptures better than many of us, and the Germans have made the text of the Bible so plain and easy with the Hebrew and the Greek that many things be understood without any glosses at all than by all the commentaries of the doctors.[2]

As the vernacular Bibles spread into the lower orders of society they became an incentive to and a vehicle of literacy and of a simpler, lay piety. In barns and mills, in forests, groups of old Lollards and New Anabaptists pored over God's Word: some of their leaders, like Hans Huth and Pilgram Marbeck became deeply skilled in knowledge of the Bible. In great churches and cathedrals men who could read, recited the Scriptures from the chained volumes to their unlettered comrades, sometimes like John Porter the tailor who is described as a "fresh young

[1] J. Knox, *Works* (ed. Laing), Vol. 1.100.
[2] Erasmus: *Epistolae* (ed. P. S. Allen), Vol. 5.3.

man" getting into rough trouble in the doing. A Catholic historian, Philip Hughes, has this striking comment on the tradesmen and their wives who formed a large part of the English martyrs under Mary.

> Through their habitual frequentation of the Bible these people have for themselves become transformed into Scriptural figures and all the drama of their lives has itself become transformed into a scriptural event, itself a continuation of the sacred story.[1]

Thus a new kind of church life and piety emerged, and despite the variations of the Protestant tradition, the common feature was a biblical orientation: Mattins and Evensong, *Kirchenordnungen*, Reformed liturgies, sectarian worship: the preaching of Puritans and Caroline Divines, for the spirituality of George Herbert and of Nicholas Ferrar stands on the Bible and the biblically saturated Prayer Book. Primers, catechisms, Christian ordinances: not least family religion where in Robert Burns' words "the priest like father read the sacred page" in noble halls and simple cottages. Despite all the fanaticism, the obscurantism, the folly, Luther was right: the goings on in darkened alleys did not do away the fact that in the market place good, common men could see a living fountain. Millions of men found in the Word of God sufficient light and truth to bring them nearer to God's holy hill. In that furious and turbulent age, as the dread horsemen of the Apocalypse rode out on their dire occasions, men with seeing eyes perceived another rider at their head, brandishing an even more effectual sword— the Word of God going forth conquering and to conquer.

[1] P. Hughes, *The Reformation in England*, Vol. 2, London, 1953, p. 275.

The Bible in the Eighteenth Century

EDWARD CARPENTER

IT has become almost a commonplace to assert that the eighteenth century discovered in the Gospels a rational Jesus; Schleiermacher, during the period of the Romantic movement, a Jesus of feeling; the nineteenth century a liberal Jesus; and the twentieth, against the background of war and revolution, a crisis or eschatological Jesus. Such an observation contains an element of truth, though Jesus is certainly greater than all these interpretations. Each, in a measure, represents one facet of a composite portrait; though this is not to claim that they are all equal in significance or insight.

Yet all such interpretations, in spite of the fact that they inevitably result from a selective attention arising out of contemporary attitudes and needs—that is to say, different generations have a quickened awareness of particular truths—presuppose the Scriptures as a unique source book.

It is always hazardous to make generalizations, especially when they are as incapable of proof as of disproof. Yet in spite of this, it may be claimed that a continuing preoccupation with the Scriptures, and a tendency to go over them again and again, are a legacy of that great religious awakening known as the Reformation. The breach with Rome, which meant the repudiation of an authority which had obtained for over a thousand years, and had given stability to a civilization, led to a revolution in man's view of society, and indeed of life generally, which it is difficult for us now fully to appreciate. Such a forthright abandonment of an ancient past, while it appeared to many Reformers as a return to a more primitive Christianity and to humanists as a great step forward on the road to man's emancipation, also brought with it a sense of insecurity, rather like the bemusement of an undergraduate newly arrived at his university. In certain respects this void came to be filled by the emergence of the renaissance Prince, himself embodying the growing self-consciousness of the nation-state and its will to power; but in spite of his seeming self-confidence, the Prince himself often felt the need of a sanction for his new position of unique and awesome responsibility.

The Bible, in protestant countries, seemed to provide just that divine support which an essentially individualistic religion and a new political order required. The new claims appeared untenable without an adequate rationale to support them. Only the Bible was big enough to furnish it. As the traditional Church had claimed to be an infallible authority, so equally must the Bible occupy no less exalted a rôle. Lutheranism, Calvinism, Anglicanism—these all regarded themselves as biblical, that is they claimed to derive their own final justification from the Word of God. Each maintained that if the supreme and unique authority of the Bible were but first recognized, then an inspired understanding of it would inevitably lead to its own particular theological system and church order—or fairly near to it. Whether it were the Confession of Augsburg or Geneva, the Heidelberg Catechism, or the Thirty Nine Articles, it made no difference in this respect, though there were varying opinions as to the value of tradition which all yet agreed was subordinate to the Scriptures. True, so far as the individual believer was concerned, he must accept the principle of *cujus regio ejus religio*, yet each protestant denomination asserted its right to exist and to propagate its beliefs on the grounds of its biblical status.

The Anglican position was no exception, though it was usually stated with more restraint and sometimes with a measure of ambiguity. Thus the Articles of Religion affirmed that "Holy Scripture containeth all things necessary to salvation: so that whatsoever is not read therein, nor may be proved thereby, is not to be required of any man, that it should be believed as an article of the Faith, or be thought requisite or necessary to salvation". The three Creeds "ought thoroughly to be received and believed: for they may be proved by most certain warrants of Holy Scripture". The judicious Hooker (1554?–1600) accepted this priority of the Scriptures as essential and axiomatic to the Church of England, though he saw the Creeds, and the continuing tradition of the Church, as conditioning, indeed as controlling, a reasonable interpretation.

Such a rational biblicism meant that most Anglican theologians of the Reformation and post-Reformation era, loyal as they were to their own Church, were not prepared to "un-Church" protestants on the Continent simply on the grounds that they had abandoned episcopacy. What in fact united those Churches which had repudiated the Papal allegiance (apart, of course, from this repudiation) was their acceptance of a common authority in the Bible. At first animosity to Rome was so strong that they did not always fully appreciate how divisive this new loyalty could become. The Word of God was pre-eminent over all. No Council, no Creed, no continuing tradition, no use of reason arguing from moral principles, could claim validity except in so far as it found "warranty" in the Scriptures. What protestants differed about was how far any of them did find such warranty. In taking this stand, all the protestant Churches differed from the Roman Council of Trent (1545–63) which decreed that "this Synod receives and venerates with equal adhesion of faith and reverence all the books both of the New and Old Testament . . . together with the said Traditions, as well those pertaining to faith as those pertaining to morals".

Such a general protestant principle, however, in an age that had not yet learnt tolerance, was bound in the nature of the case to lead to problems, particularly when animosity to Rome lessened and the struggle for survival became at first less urgent and then passed away. It was finally only the growth of a secularist humanism, following upon theological exhaustion, which kept the peace into which the eighteenth century entered.

2

It is obvious, and seventeenth-century man could not but become aware of it, that the meaning of the Bible is not always transparently clear. Roman Catholic theologians, in asserting the claims of both Church and tradition, made much of this self-evident fact. The Scriptures are indeed highly complex in character, and they range over a vast period of time. Their contents include racial memories, history, law books, poetry, prophetic utterances, letters, and so on. Such unity as this diverse material may be thought to possess most certainly does not exist in any set of unchanging and self-evidencing propositions about God. There is repetition, contradiction, development, retrogression, allegorical statement, historical narrative; and though these may all be seen as expressive of the life of a nation in its God-controlled history, yet this linking up itself supposes a way of interpreting the Scriptures which the seventeenth century was only just beginning to make. Also the quickened and critical interest in the study of language, particularly the Greek language, which the Renaissance inspired, and which led to a desire to get behind the Vulgate, meant that not only did difficulties in translation begin to obtrude, but doubts also as to the authenticity of the text. "Your pocket Bible may say so and so, but the original says otherwise" —so did a devout Anglican attempt to humble a Puritan into silence. Brian Walton's "Polyglot" (1652), and John Mill's Greek Testament (1707) with its 30,000 variants—though the latter scholar rightly claimed that this made the text even more secure—had the effect of suggesting that the original was suspect, if not doubtful, and it did this just at a time when the Bible was bearing an unparalleled weight.

What this meant was that the Reformers, in taking over the Scriptures as their final authority, had not in fact found a support which was either self-explanatory, or amenable to one interpretation only, particularly when it was translated into the vernacular, and the controlling discipline of a universally accepted Church and a regulative tradition was removed. True,

Calvin might claim in his *Institutes* (1559) that Scripture was "self authenticated, carrying its own evidence along with it, and ought not to submit to proofs and arguments, but obtains the conviction which it merits with us by the testimony of the Spirit": yet painful experience seemed to suggest that the Spirit authenticated different interpretations.

It is not, of course, true that the Bible was absolutely unknown even to the rustic worshipper during the Middle Ages, for where its ethical teaching was most simple and clear, the village priest used it for elementary moral instruction. What was generally recognized, however, in those days, though medieval theologians themselves differed as to the precise relationship between Church, tradition, and Bible, was that the interpretation of the Scriptures was a highly skilled matter; that the expertise was not attainable by every man; and that hidden deep in the pages of the divine Word were truths which had to be sought diligently as pearls of great price—depending upon meanings which were symbolic, allegoric, mystical, and of which the least important might well be a purely literal understanding. Because of this, quite apart from the almost total illiteracy of the "man in the street"—and not only him—during the Middle Ages, and the fact that no commonly accepted translation of the Scriptures existed, it was necessary that the Bible should be closed: to be opened only by those whose training and vocation fitted them to declare its message, and to ensure that no confusing controversy arose between the traditional faith and the Word of God. This basic and acknowledged assumption had successfully protected the Bible from just those popular stresses and strains to which post-Reformation biblicism now exposed it. The eighteenth century lived in the aftermath of this opening-up process and in a mood of reaction against it.

The Reformers, however, were on the whole undeterred by any sobering reflections as to how explosive and divisive the Bible could prove once the customary restraints upon interpretation, imposed for centuries, had been removed. They probably supposed that their Confessions would provide a sufficient safeguard as had, in Romanism, an infallible Church interpreting both Scripture and tradition. Certainly Luther, who was perhaps more extreme in his biblicism than any other Reformer, suffered no inhibitions on this score; and he looked forward with eager expectancy to the day when the ploughman would sing psalms as he tilled the soil. It never occurred to him that the resulting chorus might prove to be somewhat discordant.

Nor must it be forgotten that this opening-up of the Bible, and the making it bear the final burden of supporting a religious system, was effected by the Reformation at a time when the Renaissance was liberating thought and prompting ambition. The latter placed the emphasis upon the divinity that was in man, and consequently encouraged him to be critical and inquiring. The resulting intellectual climate thus brought about a great change in the way that the Bible was read and studied. When the Catholic humanist, John Colet (1467?–1519) lectured on St Paul's epistles he gave to his treatment a new look, that is a historical and personal approach which were unusual for the time. Professor Seebohm writes: "Colet sought also to throw a sense of reality and life into their teaching [i.e. of the epistles], by showing how specially adapted they were to the circumstances of those to whom they were addressed."[1] Nor must it be forgotten that the emphasis in Roman Catholicism on a continuing tradition also encouraged the growth of historical studies, as may be seen in the School of Benedictines at St Maur.

The fact that the Scriptures were now being submitted to this kind of treatment, no matter in how tentative a way, showed how strongly the winds of change were blowing. It is difficult to fence in this sort of criticism by guaranteeing its conclusions in advance. Though objectivity was the intention, subjectivism was inevitably bound to creep in.

If Roman Catholics had to ask themselves what precisely was the status of tradition, equally Protestants were forced

[1] Frederic Seebohm, *The Oxford Reformers* (Everyman ed., 1929), p. 20.

to ask what the Scriptures had laid down concerning discipline and church order. It was not always easy, in giving an answer, to avoid arguing in a circle.

In practice, however, the ethos in which these questions, in England, were raised became increasingly caught up in the psychological atmosphere engendered on the one hand by the rationalism of Descartes (1596–1650) and on the other by the successful use of induction in the world of the physical sciences. The result was to impose upon biblical interpretation a highly selective critique; and to use this critique for what were thought to be eirenical purposes. It needs to be remembered that the century following the Reformation was an era of bloody religious strife which ended by the almost complete depopulation of parts of Germany. At the same time it witnessed an investigation of the physical universe such as to suggest that here at least was order, uniformity—and for practical purposes a degree of certainty. Laymen, whose interests were not primarily speculative, began to ask themselves whether it was not possible to devise a version of the Faith which all men of good will could accept with the same assurance, and lack of emotion, as they did Newton's law of gravitation, or Harvey's thesis as to the circulation of the blood. Surely the function of Christianity was not to breed war and foster division but to promote peace and establish concord.

The new confidence which, over the years, was born in man as the result of his successful defiance of an ancient religious authority and his equally successful prosecution of scientific investigation encouraged a dynamic belief in the power of the human reason. Could not this faculty, it was asked, which one of the Cambridge Platonists designated "the candle of the Lord", discover a religion sufficiently clear as to be beyond controversy and divisive doubt? Those who were prepared to give an affirmative answer took one of two positions: though in practice the one position often led to the other and the line of demarcation was never absolute.

First, there were those who professed a rational deism almost completely independent of any particular Christian sanction. Such were Lord Herbert of Cherbury (1583–1648), brother of the devout Christian poet, and John Toland (1670–1722).

A second group, no less rationalistic, contained their rationalism within a broad Christianity, which they adjusted—often without being aware of it—to make such an accommodation possible. These thinkers emphasized the priority of the Scriptures, but it was the Scriptures understood in a special minimal way. Such an interpretation they saw as a counter-blast to the militant and exclusive claims of competing Churches and rival theological systems.

A typical example of this latter approach may be seen in William Chillingworth (1602–44) whose words came to constitute almost a battle cry: "I am fully assured", he wrote, in his *Religion of Protestants*, "that God does not, and therefore that men ought not to, require any more of any man than this, to believe the Scripture to be God's word, to endeavour to find the true sense of it, and to live according to it." "The Bible, I say, the Bible only is the religion of Protestants." Any teaching other than that which was clearly stated in the Word of God was therefore simply a matter of "opinion" and as such had no general authority.

Maybe this biblicism appears no more extreme than that of Luther to which attention has already been called. This, however, is not really true, for whereas the German Reformer asserted it to support an intensely personal and evangelical faith, Chillingworth did so in the interest of a liberal and rationalistic Christianity. Yet Chillingworth's solution of the religious problem is not quite so simple in practice as it first seems. His final interest, of course, was moral and eirenic, and he saw the Bible, when intelligently and liberally interpreted, as a means of ministering to this basic concern. To a person of such calm temper and detached reflection, the Bible understood in this way seemed all that was needed, particularly since such as Chillingworth were unaware how many other assumptions they were taking for granted. In fact, they were as much concerned to deny an authority in the Pope or in extreme sectarianism as to establish it in the Scriptures. The most effective means of achieving the first seemed to be to assert the second.

Yet it is now evident that unless there was a large measure of tolerance to begin with, together with some agreed distinction as to what was essential or non-essential in the Scriptures, biblicism of this kind could not of itself establish an eirenicum. When, for example, Thomas Tenison, later Archbishop of Canterbury, referred in 1683 to "Presbyterians, Arians, Socinians, Anabaptists, Fifth Monarchy Men, Sensual Millenaries, Behmenists, Familists, Seekers, Antinomians, Ranters, Sabbatarians, Quakers, Muggletonians, Sweet Singers" (who, he commented, "might associate in a Caravan but could not joyn in the Communion of a Church"),[1] he was well aware that these expressions of Christianity all claimed to be essentially biblical. Indeed this was the authority which each of them claimed as its own.

Here was the ambiguity. If the rationalism of the later seventeenth century led some to give priority to the Bible as itself sanctioning a more simple and less complicated faith; others of more intense and maybe more belligerent temperament saw the Bible as the begetter of new (and usually their own) dogmatisms. But the steady drift of opinion, as the seventeenth century moved to its close, was towards the first rather than the second of these approaches. This may be seen in the writings of two thinkers, both of European reputation, whose ideas exerted an enormous influence in shaping the great age of reason. I refer to Spinoza (1632–77) and John Locke (1632–1704).

Spinoza, it must be remembered, entertained an almost pathological horror of strife and persecution, and was convinced that these were often engendered by a misunderstanding of the Scriptures. Hence he has much to say about the Bible, in particular the New Testament, in his famous *Tractatus Theologico*

---

[1] T. Tenison, *An Argument for Union*, 1683, p. 4.

—*Politicus* (1670).[1] His basic contention was that "the Scripture doth teach us no Philosophy, but only Piety; and all things contained in it are fitted to the Capacity and Opinions of vulgar people". In other words, the Bible contains a revelation communicated to men in their historical situation. This means that "we are not bound to believe anything more from the Prophets, than the end and substance of what they revealed; and that in other things it is free for a Man to believe as he thinks best". Such distinctions are, of course, not always easily drawn, but Spinoza sees the "end" or the "substance" as directly related to the moral life: everything else is either uncertain or speculative, representing an accommodation to the limited mental horizon of those to whom the revelation was communicated. Equally the positive injunctions of Christ were solely intended to persuade his disciples "to live righteously"; and they must therefore be understood within this limiting context. For example, when Jesus says: "If Satan cast out Satan he is divided against himself", this must not be taken as implying that "Christ's words are an absolute proof that there are Devils and a Kingdom of Devils".

Spinoza went on to argue that it was precisely because this distinction was not recognized that the Bible exerted such little practical and moral influence on the lives of ordinary people. Unfortunately theologians were concerned with their own "fantastical opinions", which led them to interpret the Scriptures in ways contrary to "nature and reason". "To expound Scripture," he writes, "it is absolutely necessary to compose a true History thereof, that thence, as from sure principles, we may by rational consequences collect the meaning of those who were Authors of the Scriptures, that everyone (who admits of no other Principles or concession in expounding Scripture, or in reasoning of the things therein contained, but such as are fetcht from the Scripture itself, or the History of it) may proceed without danger of Erring, and be able to discourse and reason as securely

[1] The quotations which follow are taken from an anonymous English translation published in London in 1689.

of things which exceed human capacity, as of anything we know by natural light."

This leads Spinoza to maintain that there are three canons of interpretation. First there must be a just appreciation of the original languages in which the Scriptures were written, "according to the ordinary use of speaking". Secondly, the material in each book must be selected and grouped together according to its subject matter, the self-evident being separated from the obscure. Thirdly, a history must be drawn up of the lives, manners, and studies of the various biblical authors.

There is an obvious difficulty in Spinoza's argument, for if it be assumed that the method of the inductive sciences can be used to verify historic statements it is difficult to see how it can equally be used to establish that moral teaching which he regards as supremely important. Here, however, Spinoza is at one with the rationalism of his age. To him, the divine authority of the Scriptures rests upon their intrinsic moral excellence: they are (to use a modern if well worn phrase) self-authenticating in their own sphere. One cannot but suspect that Spinoza approves the historical approach when it can be employed to dispose of moral teaching and ecclesiastical claims of which he happens to disapprove. He therefore affirms with confidence: "Miracles cannot prove the Divine Nature of God . . . The Divine Authority of Scripture appears then in its teaching us what is true and real Vertue, and that can be proved only by Scripture itself; if not, we could not without a great deal of prejudice believe the Scriptures, and think them to be of divine inspiration." This is diluted Calvin.

The views of Spinoza are of interest because they represent the convictions of a deeply religious man, himself detached from any denominational Christian loyalty, yet with a great concern for his brother man. He is obviously anxious to avoid a situation in which the Bible, the great new authority of protestant Europe, can be used in the interests of a persecuting orthodoxy. The scope of the Scriptures must therefore be limited, in their practical application, to an area where there is most likely to be agreement—that is to the strictly moral life.

Equally in John Locke, it is the moral concern which has pride of place: but his protestantism is more Christian in that he ascribes a greater positive priority to the Bible. "Whoever would attain to a true knowledge of the Christian Religion in the full and just extent of it", he writes, "let him study the Holy Scriptures, especially the New Testament, wherein are contained the words of eternal life: It has God for its author, Salvation for its End and Truth without any mixture of error for its matter."[1] Such words might equally have come from the pen of John Wesley.

Like Spinoza, and equally in the interests of religious peace, Locke's first instinct is to seek in the Bible that deposit upon which all men of good will can agree. He recognizes that the Bible is not an easy book to understand since much of it is obscure, and therefore that it is obviously absurd to demand assent to every jot and tittle of it as a condition of salvation. All that can reasonably be asked in these circmustances is that the Christian should not go out of his way to dispute the meaning of perplexing passages. Fortunately what is really essential for man's ultimate well-being is perfectly simple and clear, neither more nor less than to believe in Jesus as the Messiah—and the minimum of what this entails. In a spirit characteristic of the age—and this was to be reiterated by deist and latitudinarian Christian throughout the eighteenth century—Locke writes: "The Writers and Ranglers on Religion fill it with niceties, and dress it up with notions; which they make necessary and fundamental parts of it; As if there were no way into the Church, but through the Acadamy or Lyceum. The bulk of mankind have not leisure for Learning or Logick and superfine distinctions of the Schools. Where the hand is used to the Plough and the Spade, the head is seldom elevated to suchlike Notions, or exercised in mysterious reasonings."

[1] Quoted in *A New Translation of the New Testament . . . from the Paraphrase of the Late Philip Dodderidge*, 1765.

What the Bible does is to supplement natural revelation, given through the unassisted reason, with "a new set of discoveries, communicated by God immediately, which reason vouches the truth of, by the testimony and proofs it gives, that they come from God". The biblical revelation is therefore authenticated in a thoroughly rational way, and is in this respect quite different in its general character from the "phantasies and enthusiasms of many a pretended prophet". Indeed the "internal light" can only be trusted when what it suggests conforms (*a*) to the principles of right reason: and (*b*) to the Word of God which is "attested revelation".

In respect of the latter (i.e. the biblical revelation)—and here Locke takes a view at variance with Spinoza, because he still finds room for particular Christian doctrines—the authority of those whose testimony lies behind the Scriptures does not depend on their "persuasions" ("the bent of our own minds") but upon objective testimony, "outward signs"—that is the miracles. Locke's very rationalism makes him declare that only the latter can convince us that the Scriptures are "an offspring of Heaven and a divine Original".

It will be seen that John Locke is attempting to do two things which are not easily reconcilable. He is concerned to lift the interpretation of the Scriptures out of the hands of the theological expert dedicated to a persecuting orthodoxy; yet equally to protect them from the anarchy of enthusiastic and eccentric exposition. The value of the miracles was that they seemed to have a certain "given-ness" beyond subjective argument.

What Locke says here was generally followed by later eighteenth-century expositors of the Scriptures, though with some the emphasis tended to be more on the miracles as authenticating the specifically doctrinal aspects of Christian faith, for example the atonement. In the main, however, the miracles simply guarantee the testimony of the biblical authors by making it plain that they were supported by a divine authority. In themselves the miracles have no religious value:

they are not part of saving truth; they are simply the credentials.

It lies outside the scope of this lecture to enter into a critique of this position: but it may be worth noting that it represents an endeavour either to support ethical norms by relating them to an ontology or an effort to make it rational to believe the Christian mysteries. Such an attempt must of necessity begin by assuming that ultimate value and final existence are one and indivisible.

We have quoted thus briefly from Spinoza and Locke because they were both thinkers of European reputation whose influence, during the whole of the eighteenth century, continued to be both powerful and formative. Many orthodox theologians—orthodox at least as then understood—who would most certainly not have gone all the way with either of them in his minimizing interpretation yet became imbued with much of their spirit. Eloquently in London pulpits and in cathedral churches: less eloquently, may be, in small rural churches, such exposition became a staple diet. The general tendency was to approach the Scriptures in a temper of mind anxious to prevent religion becoming more complicated than it need be. The interpretation of the Oracles of God must not be placed in the hands of an infallible Church nor, for that matter, in an equally infallible and indeed more anarchical individualist intuition. What really mattered in the Scriptures could easily be understood: and this was its morality and what relates to its attainment. Obscurity there certainly was but this need not constitute an occasion for strife.

It is worth noticing, also, that Spinoza and Locke are both dealing with problems arising from an "open Bible", and in their treatment of it they are obviously seeking the best of both worlds—to open it to their own rationalistic moralism and to close it to any other interpretation. In this respect, protestant scholars stood in a very different position from their Roman Catholic counterparts. This difference was recognized on both sides, and both tried to use it for propaganda purposes. Thus some Roman Catholic theologians saw themselves as freer to investigate the Bible critically just because the results of their inquiries could not be regarded as having any doctrinal significance. Doctrine was the exclusive affair of the Church and the Church was as concerned with tradition as with the Scriptures. Richard Simon, for example (1638–1712), in suggesting that the different sources lying behind the Pentateuch could be most easily accounted for by supposing a group of inspired "public recorders", was careful to add: "The Catholicks, who are perswaded their Religion depends not onley on the text of Scripture, but likewise on the Tradition of the Church, are not at all scandalized to see that the misfortunes of Time and the negligence of transcribers have wrought changes in the holy Scriptures as well as in prophane Authours: there are none but prejudic't Protestants or ignorant people that can be offended at it."[1]

Simon, as a Roman Catholic, is anxious to avoid personal inconvenience at the hands of his own Church by deliberately disclaiming any intention of drawing doctrinal or theological conclusions from his biblical studies. How far this kind of separation or departmentalism is possible is another matter. Certainly it was quite intolerable to Christian deists, in whom the propagandist was usually more evident than the exact and painstaking scholar.

More solid in his achievement than Simon, because living somewhat later, was another Roman Catholic, Jean Anstruc (1684–1766), who paved the way to the higher criticism of the Old Testament by being the first to discriminate between a "Jaweh" and an "Elohim" source in the Pentateuch. In doing this, he anticipated the great work of the German scholar Eichhorn (1752–1827) who came to the conclusion, as a result of his own researches, that "most of the writings of the Hebrews have passed through many hands". Eichhorn, however, is himself an example of a conscientious scholar who found it impossible to separate his academic studies from his own deeply felt convictions. A product of the enlightenment, he accepted

[1] See his *Histoire Critique du Vieux Testament* (1680).

as almost axiomatic that the miracles in both the Old and New Testaments could be explained in terms of natural principles, and that they were an expression of the superstitious beliefs commonly held in biblical days.

Yet this failure to distinguish between fact and interpretation must not be exaggerated. True, it was common throughout the whole of the eighteenth century—but not only then—yet, paradoxically, sometimes passion can help to engender insight. Pure scholarship does not exist. What matters is to be sufficiently critical to know what our preconceived ideas or assumptions are. The eighteenth century was in fact feeling its way towards following "whither the argument leads". John Spencer (1630–93) in his *De Legibus Hebraeorum* laid the foundation of the science of comparative religion: while John Mill's prodigious work on the Greek text (1707), together with the labours of Richard Bentley (1662–1742), greatest of all English scholars, bear witness to the renaissance spirit at its best.

It was inevitable that the work of such scholars should be used to provide ammunition for those whose Christianity was minimal or belligerently non-existent. Mill's Greek Testament is a case in point. Since it was the Bible, under protestantism, which occupied as a guaranteeing authority the status which the Church occupied under catholicism—each being used to rebut the claims of the other—men who longed mainly for peace sought to get behind them both. In trying to do this, they were forced to recognize that the day of the religiously neutral state was not yet and that the alternative therefore seemed to be the conversion of Christianity into a theistic religion which was content to affirm the existence of God, the need to serve him by a life of active goodness, and the existence of a future state of rewards and punishments. Some who regarded such a simple creed as "all ye know on earth and all ye need to know" lived prudently within the Church of England, tucked away in comfortable university fellowships; or they belonged to one of the dissenting bodies. Others who were more extreme, and had no emoluments to lose, made no secret of their real opinions, and indulged in a violent hostility to the Church in the interest of what they regarded as a purely natural religion.

Once again, as happened earlier in the dialogue between protestant and catholic, the debate between Anglican churchman and deist centred upon the nature and status of the Scriptures. These claimed to be an authoritative and divine revelation mediated through certain historic events and this involved a supernatural element uncongenial to those committed to an out-and-out rationalism. Thus behind the spate of solemn octavo volumes and more numerous pamphlets which were on sale between the years 1695 and 1750, there lay the final question as to the authority of the Bible, and how the biblical deposit was to be interpreted.

If this controversy may be regarded as having a beginning, since its real origins, as we have seen, lay far back, it may be dated from the appearance of John Toland's *Christianity not Mysterious* (1696). Nominally a member of the Church of England, and a self-confessed disciple of John Locke (to the latter's embarrassment), Toland went further than his master in that he would not allow to revelation any truths that went beyond reason. "I take it to be very intelligible", he writes, ". . . that what is evidently repugnant to clear and distinct Ideas, or to our common Notions, is contrary to Reason: I go on therefore to prove, that the Doctrines of the Gospel, if it be the Word of God, cannot be so." Christianity is a thoroughly rational system: indeed if it were in any sense "mysterious" it would be unintelligible, and its moral influence therefore non-existent. Christian doctrines, once revealed, are perfectly plain, intelligible, and hence reasonable. Following the lead of Spinoza and indeed of Calvin (though departing here from Locke) he maintained that "the proof of the divinity of the Scriptures is its self-evidencing power". It was the alleged "mysterious" element in the Gospel which bred controversy and strife.

It will be immediately recognized that implicit in this critique (though not explicitly stated) is an attack on the whole historic foundations of Christianity: but whereas Toland was content to write in general terms, other deists came forward who were prepared to be far more particular (and sometimes clumsy) in their hostility. Such men openly questioned the historicity and often the morality of the Scriptures. To do so they sought to employ, in a rudimentary way, the critical apparatus which more serious scholars had provided. In practice, however, their assault sprang from a rationalist and moral *a priori*.

The miracles once again were bound to receive special attention, because of the place which they had come to occupy in orthodox apologetic. The eighteenth century confronted a paradoxical situation in that the very belief in the uniformity of nature which made miracles psychologically less credible, at the same time made them seem far more significant—if their actual occurrence could be proved. They pointed, or were accepted as pointing, to a divine sanction and divine approval. Thus from Locke to Archdeacon Paley theologians endeavoured to do three things: to state precisely what end miracles served; negatively to break down the quasi-philosophical arguments against the possibility of their taking place; and positively to establish that they did in fact happen.

Paley (1743–1805), in company with many other theologians, is careful not to make the miracles bear too great a weight. They do not, for example, prove the existence of God. Quite the contrary, for to be of any value in a Christian apologetic (otherwise the argument is purely circular) the existence of God must first be established on quite other grounds. But once this is done (by the argument from "design") then the invasion of the ordered system of nature by the miraculous is a sure indication of a divine intervention for particular ends, namely to guarantee the testimony of the "revealer" or the eye-witnesses. The question whether miracles have in fact happened, since the possibility of them cannot be excluded, is purely a matter of evidence. To argue that their occurrence is contrary to experience is to limit the possible area of "what happens" to man's own limited knowledge. Natural laws are not of this kind.

This external support for Christian Faith did duty in season and out of season, and the resurrection in particular was its supreme expression. The fact that the early disciples also possessed miraculous gifts, and in addition were prepared to surrender their lives in order to give their testimony—these were seen as almost conclusive proof of the reliability of the scriptural evidence.

Such an apologia meant inevitably that attacks on the miracles were frequent throughout the century, from the crazy Woolston (1670–1733) to the philosophic Hume (1711–76). The latter's famous scepticism may be stated in a typical utterance. "No testimony", he writes, "is sufficient to establish a Miracle, unless the testimony be of such a kind, that its falsehood would be more miraculous, than the fact which it endeavours to establish: And even in that case there is a mutual destruction of arguments, and the superior only gives us an assurance suitable to that degree of force, which remains after deducting the inferior." [1] The Scottish philosopher, in the main, left it to others to draw the appropriate conclusions from this cold logic. Earlier in the century, Conyers Middleton (1683–1750) questioned, with considerable sarcasm, the credibility of the miracles alleged to have been performed by the early Church. By so doing, he undermined confidence in the Gospel miracles, although he denied any such intention.

The other external support to faith—it was usually regarded as part of the miraculous—was the prophetic element in the Old Testament, which it was claimed had been fulfilled in Jesus. It was to break down this argument that Anthony Collins (1676–1729), wrote, among other works, his *Literal Scheme of Prophecy*. In carefully guarded language, he denied that the fulfilment of prophecy could legitimately be regarded as in any way literal or historical: rather it must be understood in an allegorical sense. "It seems therefore" he wrote in his *A Discourse of the Grounds and Reasons of the Christian Religion* (1724) (and

[1] See David Hume, *An Enquiry concerning Human Understanding*: Sec. X *Of Miracles*.

there is a strangely modern ring about this), "most destructive of Christianity to suppose; that typical or allegorical arguing is in any respect weak and enthusiastical, and that the apostles always argued in the matter of prophesies according to the literal sense of the prophesies, and the way of reasoning used in the schools: since it is most apparent; that the whole gospel is in every respect founded on type and allegory; that the apostles in most, if not in all cases, reasoned typically and allegorically; and that if the apostles be supposed to reason always after the rules used in the Schools, and if their writings be brought to the test of those rules, the books of the Old and New Testament will be in an irreconcilable state, and the difficulties against Christianity will be incapable of being solved. Any that call themselves Christians, says Dr Allix,[1] should take heed how they deny the force and authority of that way of traditional interpretation, which has been anciently received in the Jewish Church."

Couched in respectful terms, as the above undoubtedly is, few could fail to see in it another attack on the historical foundations of the Faith, and by implication on the trustworthiness of the Bible. The most powerful reply, on the orthodox side, came from Thomas Sherlock (1678–1761) who had already championed the cause of scriptural historicity in his *The Trial of the Witnesses of the Resurrection of Jesus* (1729) in answer to Woolston. The main thesis in his *The Use and Intent of Prophecy in the Several Ages of the World* (1725) is to deny that the argument can be stated, as Anthony Collins seemed to suggest, in the form that "All the antient prophecies have expressly pointed out and characterised Christ Jesus". Rather it should be: "All the Notices which God gave to the Fathers of his intended Salvation are perfectly answered by the coming of Christ." The distinction is a subtle but no less an important one.

The seriousness of this effort to undermine both miracle and prophecy lay principally in the fact mentioned earlier, that

[1] A French protestant refugee (1641–1717).

many orthodox theologians used these external supports to validate just that element which was unique to Christianity when contrasted with "natural religion". Such a rationale invited attack—and once again it was around the Bible that the controversy raged.

The moral case against the Scriptures—and this had far greater urgency when the science of comparative religion was in its infancy and a literal interpretation regarded as paramount —was argued with varying degrees of good taste by some of the lesser known deists. It was the Old Testament, of course, which seemed particularly vulnerable in this respect; and this vulnerability had the effect of suggesting doubts as to its divine authority, the more so as it was usually accepted that the Scriptures were equally inspired from cover to cover. Mention need only be made of Thomas Morgan who condemned, indeed recounted with relish, the immoralities of the Old Testament: and referred to the Jews as "worshippers of a primitive deity which they carried about in a trunk".

It was left to Joseph Butler (1692–1752) following a clue in Origen—and also to Samuel Clark—to lift this discussion concerning biblical revelation into a new dimension. He admitted frankly that there *were* difficulties ("obscurities") in the Scriptures, but reminded the deists that there were equal difficulties in "natural revelation", which in spite of this was all too often and easily assumed to be simple and clear. "The only question . . . concerning the authority of Scripture", Butler writes, "[is] whether it be what it claims to be—not whether it be a book of such sort and so promulged, as weak men are apt to fancy a book containing a divine revelation should. And, therefore, neither obscurity nor seeming inaccuracy of style, nor various readings, nor early disputes about the authors of particular parts, nor any other things of the like kind, though they had been much more considerable in degree than they are, could overthrow the authority of the Scripture; unless the Prophets, Apostles, or our Lord had promised that the book containing the divine revelation should be secure from these things."[1] It was not a matter of "pre-conceived expectations" of what a revelation ought to be; but what in fact it was.

Butler, however, is at one with his contemporaries in insisting that it is its "moral value" upon which the Scriptures lay the chief stress: and that "if the Scripture account of the redemption of the world by Christ can be shown to be really contrary to [Reason] let the Scripture in the name of God be given up". But this is not so.

3

So far, in this lecture, we have been generally concerned with the climate of thought in which the eighteenth century was ushered in; and with the controversy which raged around the revealed nature of the Christian Faith. The Bible was central in this debate because it was taken as in fact the revelation itself. But this discussion largely wore itself out as the century went on its sedate way. Deism either merged itself in Unitarianism; or having had a profound influence on Anglicanism and Dissent, it ceased to be a fashionable position to hold separately.[2]

Interest turned to other matters: but this partial assimilation of Deism undoubtedly affected the way in which the Bible was interpreted and used homiletically by the ordinary parish priest whether in town or country. It is now time to see the Scriptures in this more homely context.

It cannot be claimed that, as a whole—in spite of Methodism and the evangelical revival—the eighteenth century was either particularly Bible conscious or indeed was a Bible-reading age. True, Lord Cromwell's Injunctions under which a Bible "of larger volume" must be placed in every parish church was reaffirmed in 1751, since many such Bibles were now "dog eared" and venerable with age. Yet the novelty of the Great Bible had worn off and passions were no longer aroused.

---

[1] Butler, *Analogy of Religion* (Everyman ed.), p. 146.

[2] Francis Blackburne (1705–87), Vicar of Richmond in Yorkshire, could, however, maintain in the middle of the century that the sole pledge which ought to be demanded of protestant pastors was a simple and direct profession of belief in the Scriptures as the Word of God.

The reasons for this lowering of the theological temperature have been already suggested. The religious emphasis was on practical morality; not on searching the Scriptures to prove this or that doubtful point of nice theological doctrine. Indeed, the required ethics did not depend on revelation—that is on the Scriptures—for their sanction. On this most religionists were agreed, though traditional theologians maintained that the revelation provided higher and more powerful incentives to right conduct and that Jesus communicated power. As a consequence, the preacher usually strove to present the Gospel, this meant handled the Bible, in a way calculated to appeal to the prudent self-regard which was characteristic of the age. Thomas Sherlock, speaking to the Benchers from the Temple pulpit, admitted with devastating frankness that there could be no possible reason for embarking on a life of goodness unless the compensations for such self-denial in a future life were greater than the deprivations necessarily endured here in this life.

Such a religion did not add up to a zealous biblicism: indeed the rationality of it led in another direction. Thus James Boswell (1740–95), in the midst of his debaucheries in London, records that so far as the Bible is concerned "there are many people of distinction in London who know nothing about it", and adds that it was "a strange thing that the Bible is so little read". There is not (I think) one significant reference to the Scriptures in any of the Earl of Chesterfield's letters to his son, an omission which is probably indicative of the age. Dr E. Harwood (an eighteenth-century biblical translator) complained that the Scriptures were "too generally neglected by the young and gay". Boswell regarded it as a matter of self-congratulation that he was reading his Bible regularly. Indeed so moved was he with the story of Joseph and his brethren that, to quote his own words, it "melted my heart and drew tears from my eyes". "Were the history of Joseph published by some genteel bookseller as an eastern fragment", he comments, "and circulated amongst the gay world, I am persuaded that those who have any genuine taste might be taken in to admire it exceedingly and so by degrees have a due value for the oracles of God. I have a great mind to make the experiment."[1] The clear implication of this artless entry in his Journal is that not many people in fashionable society during the middle years of the century paid much attention to their Bibles.

Such a conclusion, however, must not be understood in too dogmatic or rigid a way. There were many serious Christians who studied the Scriptures regularly as part of their religious duty. John Wesley quite clearly regarded Bible-reading as a "must", and both required and encouraged it in the early Methodists. The Scriptures, he wrote, were "a most precious System of Divine Truth. Every Part thereof is worthy of God: And all together one intire Body, wherein is no Defect, no Excess. It is the Fountain of Heavenly Wisdom, which they who are able to taste prefer to all writings of Men, however wise, or learned or holy."[2] The Scriptures embraced all departments of knowledge. "The Revelation delivers what is to be, with regard to Christ, the Church and the Universe till the Consummation of all things."

In 1755 Wesley made his own conservative but forceful translation of the New Testament, modelled on the Authorized Version. In this he ruthlessly pruned away many redundancies, so effectively that three-quarters of his suggestions were adopted by the Revisers in 1881. The overriding intention of this undertaking was to "assist serious Persons who have not the advantage of learning ... plain unlettered men, who understand only their own Mother-Tongue and yet reverence and Love the Word of God, and have a desire to save their souls".[3]

The biblical emphasis in Methodism was therefore strong from the beginning. It was equally strong in the Church of England within the small circles of evangelicalism, though not only there. Dr Samuel Johnson (1709–84), the learned lexicographer, is a case in point. There can be no doubt, as his

[1] See Boswell's *London Journal*, 1762–63, ed. F. A. Pottle, 1950, pp. 197–8.
[2] *Explanatory Note on The New Testament*, by John Wesley, London, 1755.   [3] Ibid.

Diaries, Prayers, and Annals [1] make abundantly clear, that the Doctor was an assiduous reader of the Bible, particularly during his latter years. On Easter Eve, 1761, he made a firm resolution to study the Scriptures, determining to read a prescribed portion every week. In January, some five years later, with that curious hankering after a system to which he was prone (doubtless to correct a pathological laziness) he noted that it took him one minute to read six verses. [2] In March 1771, he is renewing his resolve to go through the New Testament once a year in the original Greek. Subsequent entries make it clear that he had not lived up to his various good resolutions: but he doggedly perseveres. Thus in 1773 he confesses that he had not finished reading either the Pentateuch or the Gospels as he had planned. His intention now was to read 600 verses in the Old Testament, and 200 in the Greek New Testament, every week. Despite frequent failures and lapses he carried on; and he was on the whole somewhat gratified when in April 1772 he felt able to write: "It is a comfort to me, at last, in my Sixty third year, I have attained to know, even thus hastily, confusedly and imperfectly, what my Bible contains. May the good God Encrease and sanctify my knowledge." There were, unfortunately, still great gaps which he could not but regret. He had never yet read the whole of the Apocrypha, though he could remember, as a child, hearing of Bel and the Dragon, Susannah, and Tobit. The approach of old age, and a feeling that death was near, made him still more resolutely systematic, and in August 1784, [3] the year of his death, he made what proved one final resolution "to read the Bible more".

It would be a great mistake, of course, to take Dr Johnson as representative of his age. He most certainly was not. Yet there

---

[1] *Samuel Johnson, Diaries, Prayers, and Annals.* Ed. G. E. L. McAdam Jr, Yale University Press, 1958. The quotations which follow are from this collection.

[2] Nathaniel Scarlett in his *Translation of the New Testament from the original Greek*, 1798, estimated that it took 1 hour, 8 minutes to read the Gospel of Matthew; 1 hour 9 minutes the Gospel of Mark; 2 minutes 2 John; the whole New Testament 14 hours.

[3] He died on 13 December.

must have been many others like him: and the fact that such piety could exist in the eighteenth century outside the more emotional atmosphere of the evangelical revival shows clearly that Bible-reading could be a part of a balanced religious devotion. That it was not more widespread was undoubtedly due to the fact that the contemporary religious climate was low. Johnson may well have caught his own devotion to the Scriptures, as well as his religious preoccupation generally, from William Law's *Serious Call to a Devout and Holy Life* (1728). This minor classic greatly influenced the Doctor, who told Boswell that he picked it up at Oxford, expecting to find it a "dull book". It proved, however, an "overmatch" for him, and from that day religion became the predominant interest of his life.

The *Serious Call* is itself steeped in the atmosphere of the Bible, and Johnson doubtless remembered the shining example of Miranda of whom Law writes: "The holy Scriptures, especially of the New Testament, are her daily study; these she reads with a watchful attention, constantly casting an eye upon herself and trying herself by every doctrine that is there. When she has the New Testament in her hand, she supposes herself at the feet of our Saviour and His Apostles, and makes everything that she learns of them so many laws of her life. She received their sacred words with as much attention and reverence as if she saw their persons, and how that they just come from Heaven, on purpose to teach her the way that leads to it."[1]

Nor would Johnson be likely to forget, classical scholar as he was (for it probably cut very near the bone), the gentle irony which Law indulges at the expense of Classicus. "The two Testaments would not have so much as a place amongst his books," he writes, "but they are both to be had in Greek." Though Classicus read many commentaries on the lives of Cicero, Horace, and Homer, he would read none on the Bible.

The *Serious Call* almost certainly exerted an equally strong influence on many others who are less well known to fame. Hence the several editions through which it has passed.

[1] William Law *A Serious Call to a Devout and Holy Life*, ed. S.P.C.K., 1910.

William Law, Miranda, Classicus, Boswell, Johnson—all these were educated people. It must not be forgotten, however, that the vast majority of English people were at this time completely illiterate. As such, they depended for their knowledge of the Bible on hearing it read in church, according to the lectionary of 1662, and expounded from the pulpit; and on learning a little of it by heart when instructed on the catechism during Lent as a preparation for confirmation. True, the Charity School Movement of the earlier years of the century, and the Sunday School Movement of the later years, had enabled numbers of young people to read their Bibles—this was certainly the main purpose lying behind the labours of Robert Raikes (1735–1811)—but taking the nation as a whole the numbers affected were small. Those of the "labouring poor" who were without any education and did not go to church (and visitational returns show that there were a lot of these) in common with the more debauched and irresponsible members of the upper classes, were almost certainly abysmally ignorant of the Scriptures, though the latter doubtless could remember from schooldays smatterings of biblical teaching in an education which was heavily weighted on the classical side.

It is not surprising, therefore, that preachers early in the century, and particularly evangelicals later, did not hesitate to point out, in season and out of season, that the reading of the Bible, and the study of the Scriptures, was a religious obligation. The illiterate must therefore see to it that they heard it read: that they committed small passages to memory; that they paid attention to instruction from the pulpit (which was expected to be in the form of biblical exposition). The rich and educated must study it for themselves. Typical of such sermons is one delivered by Thomas Tenison (1636–1715) which John Evelyn, that conscientious and admirable churchman, jotted down in note form.[1]

[1] The quotations which follow have been slightly modernized both in spelling and style. See *The Diary of John Evelyn*, ed. E. S. de Beer, Oxford, 1955.

Tenison began by stressing that the Scriptures must be read thoroughly, not "by scraps and chapters discontinuously" but "so as to understand the scope of them, the several occasions upon which they were written". One book should be compared with another, and the "moral, ceremonial, prophetical, and evangelical" elements distinguished the one from the other. Such diligent and intelligent reading, he went on, was no new requirement, for it was earnestly recommended by the early Fathers, in particular by Origen, Tertullian and St Augustine. Indeed "the Devil is never more confounded than when he sees a Bible in the hand and mouth of a Christian." No one was exempted from this duty, neither kings nor princes nor even those who of necessity spent their time in their "ordinary calling". Indeed even illiteracy did not dispense from this obligation. "If he cannot read himself," he can "learn to read",[1] or "get [others to] read to him, and more duly repair to the Church where they are read." The Scriptures were of "high and indispensible importance", for in them a man can learn what he ought to do. Indeed they are "the only true infallible Oracles of God, all other books whatever, not to be compared to them . . . They only direct us in the true and pure religion, and therefore are prohibited by the Papists, lest men should discover their superstition and errors." Tradition was no alternative to the Scriptures, since the former was "uncertain and almost impossible to deliver things to us through so many ages without additions and other corruptions". For this very reason God had "ordered the Scriptures to be our guides and that being prepared by humble prayer and a teachable spirit, God would [so] enlighten us, that they should not lead us into any dangerous error but show us the way to eternal life".

Such exhortation would have formed the staple diet of many a sermon, particularly so long as it was felt that Roman Catholicism was a menace. Nearly all the translations of the Bible into the contemporary vernacular during the eighteenth century—and there were several of them as we shall see in a

[1] Archbishop Tenison founded four schools during his lifetime.

moment—set out to encourage ordinary people to read and to understand. The more evangelically-minded churchmen were convinced that all who approached the Bible in sincerity would receive grace to understand it. Thus Thomas Haweis (who himself undertook a translation) maintained that "an unlearned person . . . sincerely attentive to the Scriptures, and crying to God for the spirit of wisdom and revelation in the knowledge of Him, will be led into all saving truth".[1]

A word may, perhaps, be added at this point concerning Haweis (1734–1820) since he represents the strong and pronounced biblicism of the evangelicals generally. He himself was reading the Bible at the age of three, and his lifelong conviction was that the Bible did not simply "contain" but "was" the Word of God. To be a believer on "trust" or simply by "education" was not to have a "real possession of the Faith". For this, men must themselves "consult those sacred oracles, and diligently enquiring after the mind and will of God therein revealed . . . follow with simplicity and sincerity the path marked out to them in this sure guide to heaven". The Bible is the Christian's only rule of faith and preaching, and by the Bible Haweis understands "the Word of God alone, exclusive of all traditions and human expositions". The devout believer, though he may seek help elsewhere, will finally be taught by Christ himself. The Scriptures are inerrant, "perfectly free from all falsehood and corrupt intention". They are absolutely unpolluted by any admixture of human fallibility: therefore "every tittle of God's Word is precious and is to be preserved with sacred reverence". The men who wrote the Scriptures were but "organs and instruments" not necessarily understanding "the full meaning of what they delivered". All Scripture finally points to Christ, and is self-authenticating. "The Scriptures carry their own Divine authority along with them, and through the energy of that Spirit Who indited them, impress this full conviction on the conscience."

[1] See A. S. Wood, *Thomas Haweis 1734–1820*, 1957, pp. 117–9. See also *A Translation of the New Testament from the Original Greek*, T. Haweis, 1795.

The contrast between a biblicist such as Thomas Haweis and such a divine as William Paley could not be more pronounced. It is the gulf between the evangelical and the rationalist Christian. We must remember that during the eighteenth century there were far more of the latter than the former. It is the latter who is representative: and he lingered on into the days of Sydney Smith.

Yet if preacher and translator united to urge on listener and reader the duty of studying the Scriptures for themselves, not all were prepared to commit themselves to Thomas Haweis' optimism: particularly as he himself, following Matthew Henry (1662–1714), had resorted to a good deal of allegory as well as typology in his exposition. There were undoubtedly difficulties in the way of interpretation and hours of concentrated prayer did not always get over this obstinate fact. Locke, as we have seen, admitted frankly that there were obscurities, but his general advice was not to bother about them. Certainly he did not believe that individual sincerity would necessarily make all things plain. The new historical approach also implied that the Bible could not be fully understood by the light of nature alone, even when liberally assisted by the Spirit. Some help was obviously needed if ordinary people were to avoid pitfalls or were not to be simply bemused. Not only were there the "enthusiasts" and the "phantastical" who were likely to lead themselves and other men astray, but there were also the rationalists and deists to guard against.

In practice, however, it was not so much a guaranteed interpretation as a rationalistic temper of mind, expressive of the growing secularism of the age, which made it possible for the Bible to be "opened" without engendering strife and division. People, by and large, were becoming not so religiously interested: they shared a common practical approach, and this continued to be true in spite of the evangelical and Methodist revivals which were minority movements. Paley shows hardly any trace of their influence except that he reacts strongly against them and his *Evidences* became a textbook till well on into the next century. Thus eighteenth century sermons while they can loosely be described as biblical were in the main moralistic; and it was for moral reasons that people were urged to read their Bible. Perhaps it is significant that Parson Woodforde, whose references to his sermons are perfunctory, only records (I think) one text that he used, and this was: "Let your light so shine before men that they may see your good works and glorify your father which is in Heaven."[1] It was this universal preoccupation with "sacred affection", "rational benevolence," "sacred virtue", which made problems of biblical interpretation not particularly urgent. Roman Catholicism had ceased to be a menace, and Dissent was not aggressive. Preachers could not of course entirely ignore problems of interpretation especially since ecclesiastics have a tendency to fight battles when the war is over and to entertain fears when the danger is past. Resort to allegory and typology persisted throughout the century, though such an approach was not in harmony with the main currents of thought. Sometimes, however, it could be used, as in Origen, to get out of some moral or rationalistic difficulty. John Evelyn records a sermon delivered in a London church which drew attention to the "double respect" in which the psalms could be understood, that is as referring to David, and his personal deliverance; and as "typifying the Afflictions of our Blessed Saviour in those of David" and the Church of God throughout history. Thus the destruction of Jerusalem could be seen as representing the inevitable catastrophe which unrighteousness brings down upon itself.

Sermons like this were doubtless repeated throughout the century but a matter-of-fact and down-to-earth age would be chary of pushing this kind of argument too far. Unwisely handled, it could excite the imagination and stimulate enthusiasm. The general temper had indeed changed drastically from the day when, in the middle of the preceding century, a Dean of Peterborough could preach in Paris on the theme: "The danger of interpreting Scriptures after the literal sense". The

[1] *The Diary of a Country Parson*, ed. J. Beresford, 1926, ii., p. 118.

eighteenth century felt more secure when things were the other way round! Yet if it was chary of such interpretations, and not particularly interested in divisive biblical exegesis of too theological a character, it was conscious of difficulties where the literal sense of the Scriptures seemed an affront either to reason or to the moral conscience. The conscientious preacher, therefore, regarded it as his duty to answer such objections. The usual pattern of the sermon was to place the biblical text in its historical and factual context, to deal with difficulties, and then finally to draw some practical and moralistic lesson, leaving the congregation with a quickened sense of their immediate duty. In the course of such exposition the preacher would sometimes be bold enough to suggest a textual emendation or an alternative translation, for example that in the cursing of the fig tree the text should read: "it was not a seasonable year for figs in general."[1] The limitation of biblical interpretation to (on the whole) moral ends meant that it was rare for the preacher to put forward the claims of the Church as safeguarding such interpretation. Occasionally, it is true the man in the pew was told that "the surest interpretation of Holy Scriptures" was the "universal practice of the Church": but more usually, in opposition to Rome, that "only the Scriptures must be our rule, whatever doctrine be pretended". When the ordinary layman experienced difficulty, or was unsettled by Methodism, then he could (and ought) to consult his "spiritual guides, set in the Church whose lips were to preach knowledge". This was the constant burden of Robert Skinner's attack on the Methodist lay preacher.[2] Thus Dr Johnson advised the use of a commentary, particularly for St Paul's epistles which were difficult. If a layman insisted on interpreting obscure passages of Scripture, then it was important that he should arrive at a right judgement. Thomas Haweis believed that there was always one, and only one,

---

[1] The preacher also in this case tried to get out of the difficulty by a resort to typology. The fig tree is the Jewish nation.

[2] See *Journal of a Somerset Rector* ed. by H. Coombs and A. Bax, 1930.

correct understanding of any particular passage. His testimony is startlingly clear: "As the words of the Spirit contain one precise meaning, and to communicate His mind is the intention of the Revelation, it must be our endeavour not to leave them equivocal, but to fix a clear and determinate idea to each, in exact conformity to the Original, that the true sense may be understood which can be but one."[1]

Sometimes opinion was divided between those who were convinced that "most schisms resulted from men not duly reading the Word of God and from men's ignorance of it", and those who advised against "too much curiosity as to the decrees of God". All were agreed, however, that it was a settled obligation resting upon every man to "practice the plain duties discovered in the Scriptures". Hence rewards and punishments loomed large. As Sodom and Gomorrah were destroyed by an act of divine vengeance, so equally it might happen to London, given up as it was to gin drinking and unnatural vice. When earthquakes visited the city in 1750, many a preacher thought that the hour of destiny had arrived—much to the cynical amusement of Horace Walpole.

It ought to be said, perhaps, that the constant endeavour to treat the Bible moralistically could be self-stultifying. Thus Sir William Blackstone, who entered the Middle Temple in 1741, told Sir Thomas Inglis that the sermons which he heard "when he came as a young man to London, were . . . below the standard of the morality of Plato or Cicero . . . for all that they contained of religion, it would have been hard to say whether the preacher believed in the Koran, the Talmud, or the Bible".[2] A satirical pamphlet of about the same time, under the intriguing title, *A dialogue between the Pulpit and the Reading Desk*, indulged the same lament. "Some have indeed, great Veneration for the Fathers; but for my part, I have not. I prefer the Authority of later Times, and depend most on the

---

[1] See *A Translation of the New Testament from the Original Greek*, T. Haweis, London, 1795.
[2] J. C. Colquhoun, *William Wilberforce*, 1866, p. 110.

judgement of modern Authors." As to the Bible, it is "a stale unpolished piece of Antiquity".[1]

4

Such general reflections illustrate how it came about that the eighteenth century succeeded in taking a great deal of the mystique and the *mana* out of the sacred oracles of God. The Bible must be made to speak a contemporary language and be brought into the common light of an ordinary day. Mystical, allegorical, fanciful interpretations might be just tolerated but it was the moral teaching which was important: and this moralism was authenticated by miracles and made more urgent by a system of rewards and punishments. The Bible constituted the revelation; it was the *scripta lex*, and it supplemented natural religion.

The rationalism of the age further demanded, and in this it was at one with the more fervent religionists who revolted against its rationalism, that the Bible should be translated into everyday speech. Many undertook this self-appointed task— Mace (1729), Wesley (1755), Purver (1764), Dodderidge (published 1765 but undertaken earlier), Wynne (1764), Worsley (1770), Haweis (1795), Scarlett (1798), Archbishop Newcome (1796)—to mention by no means all. Common to all these versions—some translators, it is true, attempted textual emendations—was the desire to make the Bible more easily understood by those who found the archaisms and obsolete words in the Authorized Version a real handicap. Nathaniel Scarlett, for example ("since a very material change has taken place in our language"), drew attention to the inversion in the English order of words by attraction from the Greek text. These eighteenth century translations—some were almost paraphrases—tended to fall into two classes, the literal and the "curious". The latter were somewhat fanciful, and of these Harwood's, which the author intended to be "lively", was perhaps the most extreme. Typical is his translation of Matt.

---

[1] *A Dialogue Between the Pulpit and Reading Desk*, 1767, p. 4.

6. 7 as follows: "Think not the design of prayer is by dint of importunity to teaze the Deity into a compliance with our requests."[1] Mace follows Harwood a close second, as may be seen in his rendering of 1 Cor. 7. 36: "If any man thinks it would be a reflexion upon his manhood to be a stale bachelor ... " The most curious in its general format is Scarlett's New Testament which takes the form of a dialogue introduced by a narrator.

Different, however, as all these translations are, they all bear the unmistakable imprint of the great age of reason, and all spring out of a sense of real need. Even such serious scholars as Dodderidge and Archbishop Newcome felt that "our Governors in Church and State [ought to] favour us with a new version of the Scriptures with all possible improvements".

It is necessary, however, to conclude this brief survey of the eighteenth century by striking a cautionary note which may serve to remind us how precarious over-dogmatic generalizations can be. The eighteenth century was not quite so uniformly rationalistic as the title "the great age of reason" would seem to imply. Before it had even reached the peak of its distinctive achievement, a new current of poetical feeling had begun to flow in literature generally. Rousseau, the high priest of nature, projected into the Gospel portrait of Jesus something of his own romantic sensitivity. His words are certainly worth quoting at length:

> I will confess to you, that the majority of the Scriptures strikes me with admiration, as the purity of the Gospel hath its influence on my heart. Peruse the works of our Philosophers with all their pomp of diction: how mean, how contemptible are they, compared with the Scriptures! Is it possible that a book, at once so simple and sublime, should be merely the work of a man? Is

---

[1] Harwood, *A Literal Translation of the New Testament: being an Attempt to translate the Sacred Writings with the same Freedom, Spirit and Elegance, with which the other English Translations from the Greek Classics have lately been executed,* 1768.

See Matt. 13. 51: "After speaking these parables Jesus said to his disciples—Do you perfectly understand my meaning and intention?—they answered in the affirmative."

it possible that the sacred personage, whose history it contains, should be himself a mere man. . . . What sweetness, what purity, in his manners! What an affecting gracefulness in his delivery! What sublimity in his maxims! What profound wisdom in his discourses! What potence of mind, what subtlty, what truth in his replies! How great the command over his passions! Where is the man, where the philosopher, who could so live, and so die, without weakness, without ostentation?[1]

Here nature is beginning to take on a different guise from that which it wore in the formal, rational, abstract, propositional system of such men as Clarke, Tindal, and Paley. Feeling, romance, the cult of the primitive—these are all, paradox though it might seem, being built into the structure of eighteenth century thought. A more passionate lyricism is being sought in the East, as well as in the Icelandic, Indian, Gothic, Celtic, Eskimo—and (finally) in the hitherto neglected Hebrew culture.

This minority expression of thought and feeling, which finally realized itself in the romantic movement, made its first impact upon the study of the Scriptures through Bishop Lowth (1710–87), whose Oxford Lectures on "The Sacred Poetry of the Hebrews" were published in 1753 in Latin, and later translated into English. It was something new when a donnish professor of poetry suggested that in such literature as the Psalms, the Book of Job, and the Song of Songs, there was "mystical allegory, sublimity of expression, sentiment and passion"; and that there was real beauty in the parallelism of Hebrew poetry, which had hitherto (*qua* literature) been regarded as somewhat vulgar and uncouth.

Biblical study was beginning to take on a new look but it was left to the following century to feel the full blast of the winds of this change.

[1] Quoted: *A New Translation of the New Testament of our Lord and Saviour Jesus Christ. Extracted from the Paraphrase of the late Philip Dodderidge*, 1765. See Rousseau, *Letter to the Archbishop of Paris*, London, 1763, p. 63.

The Bible since the Rise of Critical Study

G. W. H. LAMPE

IT is clearly impossible, within my allotted space, to give a detailed historical account of the rise of biblical criticism and its progress down to our own day. The main outline of that story is, in any case, already familiar and has been often told, most effectively by a number of recent writers. All that is possible here is to try to describe certain aspects of the critical approach to the Bible and to illustrate these by reference to a few selected "moments" in the long history of the interpretation of scripture during the last hundred years. I shall take as my starting-point the publication of *Essays and Reviews* and deal almost entirely with the rise and development of critical studies in this country, bearing in mind, of course, at the same time that these studies have to a considerable extent been occupied with the assimiliation, modification, and transmission of ideas which originated elsewhere, chiefly in Germany.

Let us, then, glance first at the position in 1860. The object of those of the Essayists who dealt with biblical themes was to set the interpretation of the scriptures free. This was recognized by Hort when, declining himself to join the Essayists, he wrote to Rowland Williams on 21 October 1858: "I can go all lengths with them in maintaining absolute freedom of criticism, science and speculation; in appealing to experience as a test of mere *a priori* dogma; and in upholding the supremacy of spirit over letter in all possible applications. Further, I agree with them in condemning many leading specific doctrines of the popular theology as, to say the least, containing much superstition and immorality of a very pernicious kind."

Hort's letter goes on to say that there are serious differences between himself and the Essayists on the subject of authority, and especially the authority of the Bible, which, as he says, "would make my position among you sufficiently false in respect to the great questions which you will be chiefly anxious to discuss". He is also afraid of the consequences of "a combined open assault". " At present very many orthodox but rational men are being unawares acted on by influences which will assuredly bear good fruit in due time, if the process is allowed to go on quietly; but I cannot help feeling that a premature crisis would frighten back many into the merest traditionalism."

Nevertheless, for all his reluctance to become involved in setting up "a broad conspicuous target for the Philistines to shoot at", Hort had put his finger correctly on the object which Rowland Williams and his colleagues had in mind. It was the emancipation of the Word of God from the grave-clothes wound around it by *a priori* dogmatism and by the superstition and immorality of much popular theology. They claimed, with justice, to be reverting to the more liberal attitude of some, at any rate, of the Reformers. H. B. Wilson in his essay on "The National Church" appeals to the Anglican formularies:

> It has been matter of great boast within the Church of England, in common with other Protestant churches, that it is founded upon the "Word of God", a phrase which begs many questions when applied to the canonical books of the Old and New Testaments, a phrase which is never applied to them by any of the Scriptural authors, and which, according to Protestant principles, never could be applied to them by any sufficient authority from without. In that which may be considered the pivot Article of the Church this expression does not occur, but only "Holy Scripture", "Canonical Books", "Old and New Testaments". It contains no declaration of the Bible being throughout super-naturally suggested, nor any intimation as to which portions of it were owing to a special divine illumination, nor the slightest attempt at defining inspiration, whether mediate or immediate, whether through, or beside, or over-ruling the natural faculties of the subject of it—not the least hint of the relation between the divine and human elements in the composition of the biblical books. . . . The Protestant feeling among us has satisfied itself in

a blind way with the anti-Roman declaration that "Holy Scripture containeth all things necessary to salvation, so that whatsoever is not read therein nor may be proved thereby, is not to be required of any man that it should be believed as an article of the faith". . . . This declaration declares that nothing is to be required to be believed on peril of salvation, unless it be scriptural; but it does not lay down that everything which is contained in Scripture must be believed on the same peril. Or, it may be expressed thus:—the Word of God is contained in Scripture, whence it does not follow that it is co-extensive with it.

Thus Wilson, at any rate, believed that the aim of the Essayists was in part reactionary; it was to penetrate behind the popular biblicism of the time to a wider concept of revelation. Whether he was right in claiming the support of the Anglican Article VI for this wider concept is perhaps doubtful. H. Sidgwick annotated his copy of *Essays and Reviews* at this point: "I think the reformers meant it (i.e. the Word of God) to be coextensive with Scripture. If not, who is to draw the line?" Wilson, however, was convinced that "under the terms of the sixth Article one may accept literally, allegorically, or as parable or as poetry or legend the story of a serpent tempter, of an ass speaking with a man's voice, of an arresting of the earth's motion, of a reversal of its motion, of waters standing in a solid heap, of witches, and a variety of apparitions. . . . So the dates and authorship of the several books received as canonical are not determined by any authority, nor their relative value and importance." Consequently, he goes on, "many evils have flowed to the people of England, otherwise free enough, from an extreme and too exclusive Scripturalism".

It is this sense of bondage to the letter, not of the biblical books themselves but rather of dogmatic presuppositions lacking any firm basis, that inspired the efforts of the Essayists to induce people to read the Bible "like any other book". It was in respect of their protest against putting the Bible under the constraint of later dogmatic formulations that the Privy Council's decision vindicated Williams and Wilson when it declared that the clergy were not obliged by the formularies of the Church to believe and teach the verbal inspiration of the scriptures.

This was the principal point of the most important of the Essays, that of Jowett "On the Interpretation of Scripture". He contended for several objectives, which could be summarized under one or two main heads. Inspiration, in the first place, is something to be found in scripture; it is not an *a priori* concept to be imposed upon it. "Any true doctrine of inspiration must conform to all well ascertained facts of history or of science. The same fact cannot be true and untrue, any more than the same words can have two opposite meanings. The same fact cannot be true in religion when seen by the light of faith, and untrue in science when looked at through the medium of evidence or experiment." We must not try to harmonize scripture with later orthodoxy, and, in order to do so, practically reduce the area of inspired scripture to a few proof-texts. "The Calvinist", remarks Jowett, "in fact ignores almost the whole of the sacred volume for the sake of a few verses." In this particular instance, no doubt, he was being unfair; but he is surely right in complaining that it is not easy to say what is the meaning of "proving a doctrine from Scripture". "For when we demand logical equivalents and similarity of circumstances, when we balance adverse statements, St James and St Paul, the New Testament with the Old, it will be hard to demonstrate from Scripture any complex system of doctrine or practice." So much, we may be tempted to think to-day, for "biblical theology". Jowett, however, is more concerned to insist that the primary duty of the interpreter is to discover what the original author meant. This will save him from the literalism that fails to differentiate between history, myth, poetry, and drama, and so, for instance, misses the whole point of the Book of Jonah through its preoccupation with the dimensions of a whale's gullet. It will also save him from what the Essayists regarded as a major enemy of the Word of God: the pious allegorism which had to be called in to the aid of literalism when the literal interpretation produced nonsense or worse. Jowett pushes his hatred of allegorism to the limit. He will not admit that the scripture can at any point yield more than one true meaning. If we refuse to agree that this is so, then "we assume what can never be proved, and an instrument is introduced of such subtlety and pliability as to make the Scriptures mean anything: *Gallus in campanili*, as the Waldenses described it; the weathercock on the church tower, which is turned hither and thither by every wind of doctrine". "That the present age has grown out of the mystical methods of the early Fathers", declared Jowett somewhat optimistically, "is a part of its intellectual state. No one will now seek to find hidden meanings in the scarlet thread of Rahab, or the number of Abraham's followers, or in the little circumstance mentioned after the resurrection of the Saviour that St Peter was the first to enter the sepulchre. To most educated persons in the nineteenth century these applications of Scripture appear foolish." Yet, he complains, many traces of such follies still remain to bedevil biblical exegesis. "If, for instance, we attribute to the details of the Mosaic ritual a reference to the New Testament, or suppose the passage of the Red Sea to be regarded, not merely as a figure of baptism but as a pre-ordained type, the principle is conceded; there is no good reason why the scarlet thread of Rahab should not receive the explanation given to it by Clement."

Jowett's canons of interpretation may be summed up in his own words:

Scripture, like other books, has one meaning, which is to be gathered from itself without reference to the adaptations of Fathers or Divines, and without regard to *a priori* notions about its nature and origin. It is to be interpreted like other books, with attention to the character of its authors and the prevailing state of civilization and knowledge, with allowance for peculiarities of style and language, and modes of thought and figures of speech. Yet not without a sense that, as we read, there grows upon us the witness of God in the world, anticipating, in a rude and primitive age, the truth that was to be, shining more and more unto the perfect day, in the life of Christ, which again is reflected from different points of view in the teaching of his apostles.

The hope of Jowett and his colleagues was that, "when interpreted like any other book . . . the Bible will be a spirit and not a letter; as it was in the beginning, having an influence like that of the spoken word or the book newly found". This was, of course, on the assumption that the original meaning of the biblical books was clear and straightforward, and that, if once the surrounding mists of later dogmatic or allegorical interpretation were dispelled, the scriptures themselves would stand out plainly as a simple historical record which no reader could misunderstand, different from the works of Thucydides or Polybius only in the sublimity of the story which they told.

Hort's first reaction, in a letter to John Ellerton of 20 April 1860, was simply:

> You should read the *Essays and Reviews.* . . . Jowett is provoking as usual. I suppose he will do good to some in forcing honesty of criticism upon them, though there is perhaps not a single thought new to you or me; but his blindness to a providential ordering of the accidents of history is very vexatious. . . . R. Williams on Bunsen is R. Williams all over, and quite worth reading. I have not yet touched Wilson. C. W. Goodwin, as far as I have read, is poor enough. I read about three-quarters of (Mark Pattison), and mean to finish him some day. He is, as you say, a very odd sort of a good sort of man; perhaps as interesting as a man can be without one spark of genius.

By 11 December he was telling Westcott that the "*Essays and Reviews* have, I think, flung back into mere orthodox assertion many who were feeling their way onwards, and such views will, on the other hand, be accepted widely as the utmost now tenable". The storm of orthodox agitation, however, induced him to propose to Westcott the idea of publishing a declaration regretting the "adoption of a harsh and intolerant policy, which tends to deter men of thought and learning from entering the ministry of the Church and to impel generous minds into antagonism to the Christian faith".

Thus Hort's opinions gradually changed in favour of the Essayists. He wrote again to Westcott on 15 February 1861:

It is perhaps true that I feel the errors of the *Essays and Reviews* less keenly than you do. It appears to me tolerably certain that I have a stronger sense of their truths. Also . . . I am probably less able than you to condemn decidedly the course they have adopted in precipitating a crisis. That is, while I should myself (even if I had shared their opinions) probably have thought it on the whole wisest to refrain, I still feel that they have very strong grounds for their conduct, and I do not altogether trust my own caution. Both these considerations, however, their truths or errors and their policy, are surely beside the present question. . . . They happen at this moment to represent the cause of freedom of thought and criticism, and that fact constitutes the greater part of their claim on our strength and help. A league is forming between the Evangelicals and the High Churchmen to crush all belief not founded solely on tradition, and if possible to drive from the Church all who, whether orthodox or not, value truth above orthodoxy.

Hort's fears were amply justified. Some of the most striking evidence for what he called "the conspiracy of *clerus* and *populus* to destroy whatever threatens their repose" is to be found in the pamphlet campaign by which Frederick Temple was attacked when his appointment to the see of Exeter was announced. This happened at so late a date as 1869. The literature was mainly the work of incumbents in Temple's prospective diocese, and its virulent bigotry makes it astonishing reading. Objectionable in theory as the appointment of bishops by the Prime Minister may be, and however absurd may be the idea of the regulation of Anglican doctrine and liturgy by the Privy Council, it must not be forgotten that the clergy in the nineteenth century went far towards forfeiting all claim to be entrusted with the control, or even the leadership, of a Church that professed to respect intellectual integrity. They gave ample proof that they could not be trusted to prefer truth to orthodoxy.

It was not until *Lux Mundi*, in 1889, had been greeted with another, though less violent, storm that the opposition began to die down, apart from that prolonged reluctance of the Evangelicals to come to terms with biblical criticism, which inhibited them, as a body, from making any really significant contribution to the development of Anglican theology until quite recent times.

During that period of nearly thirty years, however, much had happened—much more than could be chronicled here. In singling out one or two of its most important aspects, we must notice the beginning, in an historically much more serious way than in Renan's *Life of Jesus*, of the quest for the historical Jesus in Seeley's *Ecce Homo*. The possibility of such a reconstruction of the "Jesus of history", based on Mark's narrative as a simple factual record, was shattered in due course by Schweitzer. At the time, however, this approach to the Gospels meant a liberation of the figure of the Carpenter of Nazareth from the prevailing tradition of Apollinarian Christology, and prepared the way in some measure for the following up by the *Lux Mundi* school of the important Christological consequences of criticism. Wellhausen's *History of Israel* was not translated into English until 1885, although it had originally appeared in 1878. It was then that English readers began to become acquainted with the revolution in the whole understanding of the Old Testament which was centred upon the transference of the developed Law to a date after the great prophets. Archaeology and literary discoveries were contributing to the revision of established notions about the relation of the biblical narratives to world history and the wider context of the scriptures: the discovery of the Moabite Stone in 1868, which showed that in a sense Yahweh and Chemosh were parallel deities, regarded in much the same way by their respective followers; the emergence, through the work of George Smith, of the Babylonian epic of Creation in 1876; the appearance of the Amarna Letters in 1887; we should perhaps also notice the discovery in 1875 of the Didache, with its very considerable effect on the generally accepted ideas about the nature and organization of the early Church.

Westcott had meanwhile been attacking the problem presented by the conflict between the idea of a revelation given once for all and a revelation which is continuous and is still going on. He held that the divine revelation is "absolute in its essence; relative so far as the human apprehension of it at any time is concerned". The revelation of God given in Christ is complete, and given once for all, but, as Westcott said, "all history and all nature are a commentary upon it". Men have the task and the duty of exploring the content of the revelation; and God is both, in a sense, the object of the human quest and also its initiator and guide. Hence inspiration is partly, in Westcott's words, "the insight of holiness, and partly its divine reward". The understanding of revelation is thus progressive; or, viewing the matter from the other side, God progressively discloses himself to man's search. This was the concept of revelation which made it possible for Westcott to say, "already we are coming to know the blessing which the withdrawal of old opinions discloses; to know, as we have never known before, that the Bible is a living book".

It may well be the case that the acceptance of the idea of revelation in and through a collection of writings of men whose human fallibility was at the same time recognized was hampered by a failure to answer the question, "What is it that they reveal?" As more and more of what had once been accepted as factually true had to be discarded—narratives in Genesis, the prophecies of Daniel as prophecies, the Pentateuch, in its present form, as Mosaic history, and so on—the tendency was to fall back on a residuum of factual statement which might still claim to be the utterance of inspired men: the "straight-forward historical narrative" of Mark, for instance, now for the first time set free from the encumbrances of *a priori* dogmatizing. There was a very general failure to see revelation in terms of divine claim—claim upon man's response of faith and obedience —rather than simply in terms of factual statement. Much positive gain had, nevertheless, emerged from the work of criticism, and this can be discerned in, for example, the last lecture of F. W. Farrar's Bampton Lectures for 1885 on the *History of Interpretation*.

If it is true that Farrar was in advance of most of his contemporaries in his ready acceptance of the new approach to the Bible which critical study necessitated, he was still in many respects typical of the attitude which was now emerging. After reviewing the work of German scholars down to the publication of Strauss's *Life of Jesus* (that "deadly attack upon the centre of Christian faith") and the reactions, good and bad, which it evoked, Farrar reminds us that "the English Church, since the days of Bede and Alcuin, has rarely, perhaps never, been in the forefront of Scriptural studies". He continues:

> The views of our theologians down to very recent times have been conservative, with a caution which has not seldom proved itself to be retrogressive. The dogma which had so long maintained the absolute, supernatural, homogeneous infallibility of every word and letter contained in the Bible, had been weighed for centuries in the balances, and never without being found wanting. Every argument and principle on which it had staked its existence had been exploded by deeper investigation. No conception more subversive of scriptural authority has ever been devised than the assertion that in the Bible we must accept everything. That notion, which so irremediably confounds the truth of God with the theological notions of men, has been responsible for crimes and errors innumerable. The canon which it maintained was indefensible; its science has proved to be childish; its ethics are tainted with hatred and intolerance; its history and chronology are obsolete; its harmonistic methods are casuistical to dishonesty; its views about the inspiration of the vowel-points, and the perfect accuracy of the text, have been covered with confusion. Wherever the systems built upon this dogma have been rejected, the Bible has become more dear and more widely understood. And yet for a considerable period the main body of the English Church, ignoring the philosophy and history of the Continent, clung with tenacity to obsolete conceptions, and failed not only to further the progress of scriptural study, but even to avail themselves of the sources of knowledge which other churches so largely used. Fifty years ago the shibboleth of popular orthodoxy was the indiscriminate anathema of "German theology".

The change which had since come over much theological opinion Farrar rightly traces in no small measure to the influence of S. T. Coleridge, especially in his *Confessions of an Inquiring*

Spirit, which was published, six years after the author's death, in 1840. Coleridge, says Farrar,

> taught his fellow countrymen to acquire their estimate of Scripture from the contents and from the claims of Scripture itself, not from the theories and inventions of men respecting it. He proved how clearly a Christian thinker could see that the various books of the Bible greatly differ from each other in value, and could yet honour the Bible as deeply as the Apostles themselves. He showed how possible it was to love the Bible as a book which contains the Word of God, and yet to read it as . . . a book which, with all its divinity, with its divine origin and divine ends, is still written by human hands for human beings, for a human eye, a human heart, a human understanding; as a book which, though written for all times, even for eternity, still refers to certain times and occasions, and must from these given times and occasions be interpreted. It was for every reason which made him prize and revere the scriptures . . . that he rejected as no longer tenable a theory which falsified the whole body of their harmonies and symmetrical gradations, and "turned their breathing organism into a colossal Memnon's head with a hollow passage for a voice".

Farrar maintains that it was in the spirit of Coleridge that F. D. Maurice laboured for years amid religious obloquy and opposition, leaving to the English Church the legacy not only of writings full of thought, beauty, and tenderness, but also of a stainless example and a holy life.

Looking back over the history of recent critical inquiry, Farrar was moved to declare:

> It has overthrown false human theories, it has not shaken so much as the fringe of a single truth. But the notion of verbal infallibility could not possibly survive the birth of historic enquiry, which showed in Scripture as elsewhere an organic growth, and therefore a necessary period of immature development. And meanwhile we have been taught of God a fearlessness which enables us to examine every critical question with tolerance and candour. We have learnt to see, not only that everything is not lost, but even that nothing is lost, if criticism succeeds in proving that the Pentateuch is composed of different elements and that the Book of Chronicles is a late and one-sided narrative,

or that there were two Isaiahs and two Zechariahs. . . . Nay, more, all is not lost if we were even compelled to make the extravagant admission that the Pastoral epistles were pseudony-mous, and that the Fourth Gospel was not written by St John. Where the Spirit of God is there is liberty.

At last, however, in the final pages of his last lecture, Farrar has to come to the question, how in fact is God's Word to be discerned in these writings, and on this he has little to say except pulpit rhetoric, apart from one criterion: that the test of the Word of God is the teaching of Christ, the Word Incarnate. Farrar does not apparently consider the question of the authenticity of the *verba Christi*. Like almost all English exegetes of the period, he confines the discussion of historicity and authenticity to other parts of the scriptures, and the Gospels, or at any rate the Synoptic Gospels, are for no explicit reason exempted from the process of historical criticism. The impact of criticism on the tradition of the words of Jesus was scarcely felt until the Christological problem of the human ignorance of Jesus, raised by his ascription of Old Testament books to Moses and David, was dealt with by Gore. Farrar therefore concludes:

And if any man ask, "How are we to discriminate between that which in the Bible ought to be to us the immediate word of God and that which, having been but relative and transient, is not his word to us?"—I answer that not only is there not the slightest practical difficulty in doing so, but that the question shows, surely, a strange and unworthy timidity. In the first place, no theory which can be invented will give the certitude which is claimed for every petty detail of sectarian dissidence or theological terminology; nor can any pretence of an infallible decision ever give infallibility to hosts of fallible and varying interpretations. But for all essential truths, have we nothing to guide us into certainty? Have we no reason, lighted by God and lighting us to God, *res illuminata, illuminans*? Have we within us no voice of conscience, that aboriginal Vicar of Christ . . .? Have we no Spirit of God to guide us, or has he abdicated his office since the days of St John, or at any rate since the days of St Augustine? . . . Is it not an absolutely plain and simple rule that anything in the Bible which teaches or seems to teach anything which is not in accordance with the love, the gentleness, the truthfulness, the purity, of Christ's gospel, is not God's word to us, however clearly it stands on the Bible page?

Two things may strike us here: Farrar's principle that Christ, rather than the Bible, is God's Word, even though for him Christ's words to us can be assumed without further question to be identical with the written words of the evangelists, and his gropings towards the realization that nowhere in this life can we find infallibility. He was beginning to see that God's Word is not to be discovered except as informing the fallible thoughts of limited and sinful men. One other point in Farrar's vigorous praise of criticism has already been mentioned: his insistence on the disastrous consequences of the "all or nothing" attitude to the Bible. If all has to be accepted as an integral part of God's revelation, or everything discarded; if, that is to say, the claims of Jesus stand or fall with our acceptance of every detail of the Gospel narratives, even the contradictory dating contained in the story of the cleansing of the Temple (Farrar, of course, does not use this example, since he scarcely considers the criticism of the Gospels themselves), then the only solution for the intelligent reader would be to jettison the claim of Jesus in the manner of Robert Elsmere, and replace the Christ of faith by the human prophet, the leader in social righteousness, whose teaching would nevertheless, as Mrs Humphry Ward believed with typical Victorian credulity, be recognized immediately as superior to that of any other teacher and fill the working men's institutes of East London with enthusiastic congregations, hungry for a humanistic righteousness.

Much had thus been done, before the publication of *Lux Mundi*, to establish certain recognized results of the critical movement. These may be briefly summarized.

The Old Testament had largely been delivered from the bondage of a narrow conception of prophecy and fulfilment. It could now be read as literature worth reading, from the religious point of view, for itself and not simply as a series of disguised previews of the New Testament.

The moral difficulties of the Old Testament had weighed heavily on earlier exegetes. The conventional method of dealing with them had been by the arbitrary and artificial use of allegory, though C. C. J. Webb, in *Religious Thought in England from 1850*, reminds us that Mansel had been inclined to believe that the suspension of the laws of nature in miracles might perhaps have a parallel in the suspension, in God's good providence and for special purposes, of the moral law as well. The idea of progressive revelation, insisted on by Westcott and developed in *Lux Mundi*, went far to remove these difficulties. "The Bible would be incomplete", said A. V. G. Allen, "if it did not include the traces of childhood's faith as well as the matured experience of the perfect man."

The new approach had made it impossible, or should have made it impossible, to treat the Bible as a vast collection of proof-texts, available to fortify any and every kind of argument. It also followed from the critics' discovery of the variety of the biblical writings, of the standpoint from which they were written, and of the purposes for which they were intended, that a strict adherence to the principle that the original author's meaning is what the interpreter must primarily seek to recover made it impossible, except to a very limited extent, to use scripture to interpret scripture. To expound one part of scripture in the light of another, without regard for the differences of outlook and intention between the different authors, was a dangerous undertaking. No doubt, the nineteenth-century critics ignored a good deal of the underlying unity binding together the different writers. They tended to pay insufficient attention to the continuity of certain fundamental themes in Hebrew religion which can properly be traced through the various books: themes such as that of the covenant and election, which are in fact taken up and developed by the New Testament. At the time, however, much had been gained in setting the biblical books free from an artificially imposed uniformity.

One particularly valuable result of the critics' work is to be seen in the way in which the work of St Paul begins to take on new life. To a large extent the Apostle had been treated as though he were an academic theologian, a dogmatist whose writings could be used as a quarry for systematic theology. The work of J. B. Lightfoot had laid a foundation for a new understanding of St Paul in the actual situation of his own times, an individual missionary grappling with concrete problems and working out his theology in relation to the pressure of circumstances.

On the other hand, the tendency towards an excessive fragmentation of the biblical writings, making it difficult at times to see why they should continue to be bound up together in a single volume, was counteracted to some extent, among the *Lux Mundi* group and their successors, by a revived sense of the continuity of Church and Bible, or rather of the place of the Bible within the life, worship, and teaching of the Christian society. The emphasis laid by Gore and the High Churchmen of his time upon the continuity and, in a sense at least, the identity, of Jesus and the Church offset to some extent the dissolution of the unified biblical record as it had been understood by pre-critical dogmatists.

The outlook of Gore and his colleagues has often been described and discussed, and its bearing on this subject has been most ably set out in the Archbishop of Canterbury's recent book, *From Gore to Temple*. I therefore intend to pass it over, pausing only to call attention to two features of their thought. One is the evolutionary interpretation of the Incarnation, so central in Illingworth's essay on "The Incarnation and Development". This essay was not directly concerned with biblical interpretation, but it contributed indirectly to the acceptance of the evolutionary principle in biblical criticism, which produced the misleading theory of continuous progress in the biblical history from lower to higher levels of religious thought, and the idea of the biblical writings as the completion and fulfilment of the religious aspirations of many peoples, Hebrew and non-Hebrew alike—an idea which might seem to fit in admirably with such critical work as that of Robertson Smith in *The Religion of the Semites*.

The other and more important feature of *Lux Mundi* was its raising of the Christological aspect of the problem of biblical criticism. On the one hand, Christological considerations might seem to inhibit the free progress of criticism: if Christ attributed Psalm 110 to David, then David must be its author, whatever might otherwise be indicated by literary criticism. Alternatively, biblical criticism would compel a revision of Christology at a vital point, demolishing the strongly Apollinarian doctrine of Liddon and Pusey. The discussion of the kenotic Christologies which found their starting-point in the human ignorance of Jesus is by no means concluded yet, as witness Dr Vincent Taylor's re-examination of the matter in *The Person of Christ in New Testament Teaching*; but this lies outside our province. The heart of the matter was well expressed by R. H. Hutton in *Contemporary Thought and Thinkers*, cited by H. G. Wood in *Belief and Unbelief since 1850*:

> A divine revelation through a . . . human nature is impossible without involving human error. . . . I should as soon expect our Lord to have understood in his human intellect . . . the astronomy of the age as to have understood and corrected the scholarship and literary criticism of the age. But does it follow from this that the divine nature was not manifested in such a human nature in the only manner in which God *could* be manifested in the life of a given age and race and country—that is by a perfect personal fusion between the human nature whose conditions God had assumed, and the divine nature which had assumed them?

We may notice in passing that Hutton's rhetorical question was by no means always answered in the negative. Stubbs' Second Visitation Charge in the Diocese of Oxford (1893) declares that:

> His omniscience is of the essence of the personality in which manhood and Godhead united in him. With this belief I feel that I am bound to accept the language of our Lord in reference to the Old Testament Scriptures as beyond appeal. . . . Where

he speaks of David in spirit calling him Lord, I believe that David in spirit did call him Lord, and I am not affected by doubts thrown on the authorship of the 110th Psalm, except so far as to use his authority to set those doubts aside. . . . I cannot bear to anticipate a day when the Church shall cry out to Jesus of Nazareth, "Thou hast deceived me and I was deceived"; or to the unknown and unknowable, "Why didst thou let him deceive himself and us?

Nevertheless, the effect of *Lux Mundi* was to make biblical criticism respectable, save in the eyes of the more extreme conservatives, especially Evangelicals, and to link it with an optimistic evolutionary theology with the Incarnation as its basis and the idea of social progress as its hope. When theological thinking was dominated by evolutionary and Pelagian presuppositions, interpreting redemption in terms of an inadequate realization of human sin, it is not surprising that criticism should enter a somewhat barren phase. The earlier hopes that through the new freedom of interpretation God's Word would be heard more plainly were scarcely fulfilled. On the contrary, the idea of the Word of God was often strikingly absent from the thoughts of those who patiently toiled, through source-criticism, to uncover a solid core of history in or behind the Gospels.

That dismally pedestrian stage in biblical scholarship has been dramatically transformed, in ways which are familiar to us all: Schweitzer's abrupt transference of the kingdom of God from the sphere of social ethics to that of futurist eschatology; the rise of form-criticism, teaching that what the Gospels give us is the picture of Jesus formed by the faith of the early Church (we see him only through the eyes of the preachers, teachers, and others in the community); and the almost simultaneous insistence of Barthian theology, and later, in a different mode, of Hoskyns in this country, that in scripture the Word of God encounters men in sovereign majesty, in judgement, and in mercy. Form-criticism has led on to a renewed appreciation, first of the importance of the early *kerygma* (with perhaps an exaggerated idea of how much we actually know of the really primitive *kerygma*) as the basis of the Gospels, and secondly to a new sense of the importance of the evangelists, not as compilers, but as creative artists and theologians. Dr Ramsey touches on some of these matters, and continues: "The rediscovery of the Church within the Bible, and the Bible within the Church, carried many Anglicans far away from the apologetic liberalism or apologetic catholicism of an earlier generation; and many became aware that a similar discovery was happening in other parts of Christendom. . . . It is no exaggeration to speak of the recovery of the Bible. Those who have as theologians known the second, third, and fourth decades of this century have experienced changes easier to feel than to describe."

If the development of criticism in the past century has taught any notable lesson, it is surely this: that God speaks to us in a manner congruous with the Incarnation itself, through human words and human minds conditioned by the circumstances of place and time, subject to our ordinary limitations. They are human minds peculiarly able, as our experience and the collective experience of the Church can testify, to discern the true spiritual significance of history, which is to say that they are inspired; but they are none the less liable to error and ignorance. There is no mechanical inspiration of the words they use, and we must beware of any attempt to find a substitute for verbal inerrancy in the idea that the images in which their thoughts are given pictorial expression, the numerical or other symbols that their imagination employs, their discernment of typological correspondences, or the structure of Hebraic language and the psychology of its thought-forms are a specially designed instrument for the direct utterance of the voice of God. All these things are of the highest importance for the understanding of what the biblical writers have to tell us—much more important than Jowett or F. W. Farrar would have been willing to allow. They do not, however, form a direct channel of divine inspiration, and the "images" which guide the thinking of the prophets and poets of the scriptures are no more exempt from human error and limitation than their words.

Christ remains the true Word of God, and it is in so far as men speak truly of him that the Word is mediated to us. Those who seek some kind of infallibility and, above all, those who try to evade the historical problem of whether, and if so how far, the tradition embodied in scripture does speak truly of Christ, are tempted to have recourse to one of two possible ways of evading the issue. They may shut themselves up within the comfortable confines of a "biblical theology" that recreates the old dogmatisms from within the Bible itself, instead of imposing them from without, but which does so at the cost of slurring over the differences between the biblical writings, forgetting their context in the circumstances of their time, ignoring the question which the historian must always ask, "Did this or that actually happen?", and evading the task of relating the thought of the biblical writers to that of our own day. Those who take this course are, in effect, pretending that the century of criticism has never happened, and that what they are pleased to call the post-critical age is virtually the same as the pre-critical.

Alternatively, they may evade the same problems by a different route, and, with Bultmann, cut contemporary faith loose from its historical moorings, preserving only a tenuous connection with a *kerygma* which itself lacks any demonstrable link with actual events. This attitude involves much more than translating the gospel out of the mythological thought-forms of the pre-scientific age. It is concerned with the much more far-reaching question whether faith can ever be made to depend on historical fact. Even the most conservative preachers often say: "The obscurities or even the apparent contradictions that there may be in the Easter stories do not matter. The truth of the resurrection does not depend upon the evidence for an empty tomb or appearances to disciples; the witness to it lies in the experience of the believer when he encounters the risen Christ here and now, and enters into a foretaste of the resurrection life with him." Ought we to go on from that point until we reach agreement with Bultmann that if this is so it does not matter whether the resurrection as an historical event ever happened? And, if historical judgement is irrelevant in this case, should we extend the principle to the whole gospel and give to the alleged history a symbolical value only? Or is it not rather the present task of criticism to map out a third way, where history is respected, and where the idolatrous craving for certainty and infallibility as against probability is put aside, whether it be the certainty of a cosy biblicism or the certainty of existential encounter which has no need to look to scriptural documents or to the history that lies behind them?

The Lessons of the Past for the Present

D. E. NINEHAM

I WANT to suggest first of all [1] that the lesson of the past for the present is, in one sense at any rate, negative. By that I mean that the past has no single, consistent, or clearly formulated doctrine of the Bible, or way of approaching the Bible, to hand on to us, comparable to the universally accepted formularies it proposes for our acceptance with regard, for example, to the Trinity or the Incarnation. Indeed, to judge from the lectures we have heard, the past seems to say that each age must work out its own approach to the Bible if it is to win from it a gospel fully relevant to the contemporary situation.

One point in this connection perhaps deserves to be emphasized. Quite deliberately, the contributors to this series were asked to speak not so much about the theory of biblical inspiration in each period as about the way the text was in practice handled in order to win a relevant gospel from it. All the lectures have in fact been on that subject, and they have surely shown that this distinction between the theory of biblical inspiration in any age and the practical approach to the Bible is a real one. And if it is, it is clearly an important one. No doubt the theory of biblical inspiration has to some extent changed from time to time in the course of Christian history, but the point I want to make is that there has in fact been much wider variety than such fairly limited changes might suggest. For theologians who held an identical, or closely similar, position, so far as the formal theory of inspiration is concerned, might differ so widely in their practical handling of the text and in the methods of

---

[1] As delivered this lecture began with a tribute to Dr Norman Sykes. See Preface, p. viii.

exegesis they employed, that any impression of a common approach to the Bible would be largely illusory. For example, a theory of plenary inspiration was a very different thing in practice, when combined with the extreme allegorism of some of the Alexandrian Fathers, from what it was when combined with the literalism of some of their Antiochene contemporaries, or still more, with that of some post-Reformation theologians. I shall say no more about that, because I have made the point elsewhere, and it has been fully explored by Father Hebert and others, but it seemed worthwhile just to raise the question how far these lecturers have borne out any such contention; for if it is justified, it is clearly of the greatest importance.

It is often pointed out that, at any rate as far as Anglicans are concerned, nothing is laid down by ecclesiastical authority about the sense in which the Scriptures are inspired or the way they must be searched for religious truth; and so freedom exists for manoeuvre. But do not the previous lectures in this series suggest something which goes beyond that? If it is true that each age of Christian history has in fact—whether consciously or unconsciously—had to work out its own approach to the Bible in the light of its peculiar circumstances; and if, as we know to be the case, our age differs culturally from all previous Christian ages infinitely more than any one of them differed from any other, does the past not say to us in effect: "You must work out your own way of approaching and handling the Bible, and, in the circumstances, you must expect that your way will differ markedly from any way that has been known or practised before"?

That is not meant to suggest that, in our approach to the Bible, we shall not constantly need to learn from the past at innumerable points; it is designed, as to some extent the whole course of lectures was, to help those who, on the one hand, find themselves driven towards certain conclusions about the Bible, but, on the other hand, feel guilty about those conclusions, or even refuse to draw them, because they seem different from those of the Christian past, and so, it is felt, cannot be the right ones, even in the twentieth century.

Can we then, freed from the wrong sort of constraint by the past, face the question of the right approach to the Bible in the mid-twentieth century?

The first point to be made, although it is of quite cardinal importance, can be made quite briefly because it is by now very widely accepted in theological circles; indeed Dr John Robinson has gone so far as to say that it may well turn out to be one of the "assured results" of modern scientific theology.[1] It has often been thought in the past that being a Christian means holding a certain series of beliefs and behaving, or refraining from behaving, in certain specific ways. Along with this has gone an understanding of the Bible as the source-book from which Christians derive their characteristic beliefs and ways of behaving—a collection of inerrant propositions and irreformable demands and prohibitions, guaranteed by their direct divine origin as timelessly valid and universally binding.

Previous lecturers have described the difficulties to which such views gave rise and the attempts which were made to meet them, and I have no intention of repeating what they have said. But I should like to emphasize how long-lived this attitude was and how deep-seated it has become. Those who, from the second century onwards, allegorized the biblical statements in the hope of saving at least the figurative sense as timelessly valid; those who, in Calvinistic circles, for example, insisted on the literal acceptance of certain biblical statements— those relating to the so-called "plan of salvation"—at the expense of implicitly ignoring the rest;[2] even those liberal modernists who in effect "anthologized" the Bible—frankly jettisoning many of its statements in the belief that the rest would vindicate themselves as "timeless truths" about the

[1] J. A. T. Robinson, *In the End, God* ... p. 30, n. 1; he cites in support W. Temple, E. Brunner, J. Baillie, and A. Richardson.
[2] Cf. the remarks of Jowett quoted by Professor Lampe on p. 128; no doubt Jowett was deliberately exaggerating, but passages could be quoted to show that he was not being altogether "unfair".

relations between God and man; all these in their various ways subscribed to the sort of view of the Bible I have been describing.

And that view is by no means dead to-day. Anyone who takes part in the meetings of the synods of the various Churches as they attempt to lay down "the biblical norms" of orthodoxy and Christian behaviour must be aware that such views are very much alive. And is not each one of us aware of it in his or her own experience? When we read of doubt being cast on the accuracy of some biblical statement, do we not secretly feel that one more nail has been knocked into the coffin of biblical inspiration?

Yet modern study of this subject suggests that in large part such fears are groundless. Scholars to-day agree with surprising unanimity in questioning radically the whole approach I have been describing, and in substituting for it both a different definition of what it means to be a Christian and a correspondingly different approach to the Bible. Most theologians to-day, if asked to give a brief definition of Christianity and Christian faith, would probably define Christianity in some such terms as "putting your whole trust in God for life and for salvation"; and, with regard to faith, of the three traditional elements in it, *notitia* (knowledge), *assensus* (assent), and *fiducia* (trust), they would emphasize the last (trust) while not, of course, ignoring the others. This arises from the contemporary understanding of the Bible. There would be widespread agreement to-day that what God sought to reveal to the people of the Bible, and through them to us, was not a set of timelessly true propositions, not even propositions about himself, let alone propositions about cosmogony and astronomy and such matters, but quite simply himself; and in particular his character as a God who invites men to rely on him—or rather, demands that they should rely on him—entirely, for their well-being both now and hereafter; and who richly rewards such reliance.

I do not want to suggest for a moment that that way of looking at the Bible settles all problems—I am far indeed from thinking that—but I do want to suggest that many of us have not yet begun to take this new approach and its implications really seriously, and that it is for that reason that our thinking about the Bible is often befuddled and bedevilled by what are in effect pseudo-problems. In any study it is of the first importance to diagnose correctly what the real problems are, and if, in this lecture, I can help somewhat in that connection, I shall be more than satisfied.

It does at any rate seem to be true that as soon as we accept the new way of looking at things, the Bible falls into a new perspective. The very fact that there *are* Christians—people who seek to put their whole trust in God for life and salvation—is evidence that something must have happened to make such a response a live option for them. How did these people come to suppose that there is a God who invites, demands, and repays trust? How do they know what trusting him means and involves, and how have they been able to give content to the words "life" and "salvation"? Their very existence and way of responding to life presuppose that God has made himself, and his demands and promises, known; and the Bible claims to be the account of the occasions on and through which he has done it. That may at least serve to plot the general position of the Bible on the map of modern Christian life and thought.

And you will notice I say the Bible is the record of the *occasions* on which God has revealed himself; it is vital to understand the way in which he has worked. He chose to make himself known to mankind by addressing specific demands, promises, and self-disclosures to particular people in particular situations at particular periods in history. That meant that if his demands and promises were to be intelligible, they had to be related to the particular circumstances and cultural environment of those to whom they were addressed. Exactly how God broke through to these people we shall discuss in a moment; but whatever the method, we have no reason to think that in the process he overrode their freedom or integrity as human beings. We believe that he made available special illumination to enable them to understand what he was saying to them—

that is part of what we mean by the inspiration of the Bible—but he did not transform them into automata or force such illumination on them. Inevitably the result was:

i. that they were bound to express what they heard, or thought they heard, from him in terms of the thought-forms of a particular culture and stage of human development;

ii. that God's self-disclosure to them was often obscured and distorted by their wilful refusal to accept his illumination and understand fully what he was saying to them; or if they understood, by their sinful failure to respond appropriately.

In fact we might put it that God's method of self-disclosure to mankind was by means of a sort of dialogue with a series of historical individuals, a dialogue in which God addressed himself to the peculiar circumstances of the particular individual and his contemporaries, a dialogue in which the human participant's understanding and response were always bound to be conditioned by the cultural context in which he lived, and were often bedevilled by his moral imperfections. It is true that in the earthly life of our Lord this process of dialogue reached perfection, in the sense that the line of communication between the Father and the Son was not blocked by any sinful obstruction on the part of the Son; but even here, as H. J. Cadbury will never let us forget, if Jesus' humanity was to be real, his understanding and response in the days of his flesh were bound to be in terms of the customs, presuppositions, and logical procedures of one particular period and one particular cultural milieu. (I think, for example, of his use of such highly particular concepts as "Messiah", "Son of Man", and "Kingdom of God", or of his "furious use of *a fortiori* argument".[1]) And there is the further point that the character of his perfect response was always liable to distortion by the sinful men who first recognized it as revelatory and transmitted the memory of it to us.

That God should have chosen this mode of revelation suggests

[1] G. K. Chesterton, quoted by H. J. Cadbury, *The Peril of Modernizing Jesus*, p. 58.

many reflections. Our increasing appreciation that the use of words is always correlative to particular contexts may incline us to feel that, given the conditions of the created order, God could hardly have proceeded in any other way, but that should not prevent us from recognizing with Father Lionel Thornton[1] what supreme condescension on the part of God is here involved.

Let us be quite clear what is being said. If I may be allowed, without suspicion of irreverence, to use a rather bizarre illustration, I think perhaps I can make it a little clearer. Some of you are probably familiar with André Obey's play about Noah. It is many years since I saw it, but my recollection is that at the beginning of the play Noah appears alone on the stage with tablets and stylus, taking down from God the specifications of the Ark. One notices first that the specifications themselves presuppose the cultural conditions of the day. A wooden vessel is envisaged—it would have been no good talking to Noah of steel plates. And the measurements are given according to the standards of the time—it would have been no good talking to Noah in terms of English yards or French metres. And then it is made clear that the line of communication is far from perfect—Noah frequently cups his hand to his ear in order to be able to hear better, and keeps asking, with a puzzled frown on his face: "What was that, Lord? I'm afraid I didn't quite catch the last bit", and so on; so that one is left with the impression that what finally finds its way on to the tablets may not by any means be precisely what God originally intended. In this case of course the content of the divine demand is so precisely specific as to be readily intelligible, and the rest of the play suggests that Noah was entirely faithful, even in the teeth of much opposition, in carrying out his instructions, as he understood them, to the full. But allow for the fact that often the divine communication was not so easily grasped, and was also of such a nature that strong forces in human nature made against its full implementation,

[1] Except where otherwise stated the allusions to Father Thornton throughout the lecture refer to his trilogy *The Form of the Servant*, and in particular to the first volume of it entitled *Revelation and the Modern World* (Dacre Press, 1950).

and you get perhaps some inkling of what I mean by this process of divine-human dialogue through which revelation was given.

I ask you to notice especially in this connection the truth expressed in Father Thornton's statement that "revelation is always given not only to, but also in and through response".[1] It is through the way men acted in response to divine communications as much as through their attempts to describe those communications that the divine self-disclosure occurs. But men's response, as we have seen, was often imperfect and sometimes totally negative. In such cases God had to deal with the resultant situation through a further intervention; and so the continuing process of divine-human dialogue went on, each divine demand creating a situation which formed the background— positive or negative—for the next, and all these situations together providing the framework within which the perfect response of Jesus was possible and intelligible.

It hardly needs to be emphasized that such an account of the Bible presupposes an amazing willingness on God's part to allow his self-disclosure to be mediated through human apprehensions of it, and responses to it, which were often far from perfect.[2] The revelation was through words and actions, but there is no question of God's taking steps to ensure that every statement or action which was to be a vehicle of revelation should be precisely designed to express the divine mind—even the divine mind for a particular situation.

Father Thornton is one of those who have most explicitly drawn attention to this aspect of God's revelatory activity, and in doing so he has used the language of κένωσις or συγκατάβασις ("condescension") to describe it. Provided it is not too far pressed, this seems to me a very illuminating analogy. It has often been suggested of recent years that the idea of κένωσις—understood in a general sense—has a wider application than simply to the theology of the Incarnation; for example to God's

---

[1] p. 208.
[2] Cf. the first words of R. H. Hutton quoted by Professor Lampe on p. 140.

activity in creation and the providential ordering of the world. And certainly its application in the present context seems peculiarly enlightening. Just as its use in connection with the Incarnation can release us from a number of pseudo-problems which arise from false expectations of omniscience and omnipotence on the part of the incarnate Christ, so its use here can release us from false expectations of inerrancy and timeless validity in connection with the statements of the Bible. If Jesus could be in very truth the incarnate Son without being omniscient and omnipotent, the Bible can surely be the self-disclosure, or word, of God without its statements, even its statements about God, being inerrant or timelessly true.

As I hinted earlier, I am far from thinking that this sort of approach to the Bible disposes of all problems; many of the old problems remain, and possibly some new ones are raised. In the time at my disposal I shall only be able to glance at one or two of the problems involved. First the problem of historicity.

Here it seems to me the new approach does, to some extent, set the matter in a new and rather less forbidding light. According to the biblical writers themselves, the way the divine communication reached them was usually through the interpretation they were led to put on some historical event—it might be public or it might be private—which they came to see as manifesting the divine power and purpose in a special way, and as embodying some divine demand or challenge and inviting an appropriate response from them and their contemporaries.

It is frequently claimed by Christian apologists that the involvement of revelation with genuinely (and in many cases verifiably) historical events is something which distinguishes Judaism and Christianity among world religions, and moreover is a ground for regarding them as superior to all the others. I have no wish to deny either of these claims; so far as the claim of distinctiveness goes, I am not sufficiently well versed in the comparative study of religions to have any right to dispute it, and, as for superiority, I can see the force of such arguments as those put forward by C. C. J. Webb, for example, in his *Studies in the History of Natural Theology*[1] as showing that "it is a mark of higher development in a religion to emphasize this element [of sacred history]". But that said, Dr T. A. Roberts' recent book [2] has emphasized the need which some of us have long felt for caution in this connection and for care in thinking out exactly what it is we can and should claim.

Books on apologetics sometimes come near to suggesting that if some historical event which a biblical writer interpreted as revelatory can be shown to have happened, that is in some sense "proof" of the revelation. When the argument is stated as baldly as that, a very little reflection suffices to uncover the fallacy lying behind it. To take the crucifixion as an example, historians may provide good grounds for thinking that a man called Jesus really was crucified outside Jerusalem in the earlier part of the first century, perhaps in very much the circumstances suggested by the evangelists. If so, that will of course serve to establish the credit of the evangelists and show they were not mere romancers; but it will do nothing to settle either way the question of the status they accord to the crucifixion as a revelatory action of God and their interpretation of it as the work of God in Christ reconciling the world to himself. The truth or otherwise of that interpretation is not susceptible of being determined by the procedures of the historian.

But surely, it may be replied, many of the events described by the biblical writers are of such a remarkable character as almost to demand interpretation as special divine interventions in history. If they happened as described, there may be something in that, but at this point Dr Roberts—building no doubt on an earlier work by F. H. Bradley—brings forward a rather subtle, but highly important, point. The remarkable character of the events in question is no proof that they did not take place, but it does mean that it is impossible for the historian, *qua historian*, to decide whether they took place or not. The reason is that the scientific historian's whole procedure rests on the basic assump-

[1] p. 29.   [2] *History and Christian Apologetic*.

tion that the universe, and society within it, possess sufficient uniformity to exclude the possibility of any pronounced deviation. It is important to see that this assumption is not an arbitrary prejudice or presupposition of certain anti-religious historians; it is an assumption which every historian is compelled to make, because it is the presupposition of all his procedures as an historian. To give just one example, and that grossly over-simplified: consider, for a moment, an historian attempting to decide whether, in a particular campaign, a certain general marched an army of a certain size across a certain tract of desert, as he is alleged to have done. The historian concludes that he did not do so in view of the number and size of the oases in the desert concerned, which could not possibly have provided sufficient water for even a tenth of the number of troops supposed to have been involved. The conclusion seems sound enough, but of course it presupposes that the oases in question were producing at the particular time roughly the same amount of water they are known to produce at all other times. If the historian could not assume that, he would have no criterion, no basis for accepting or rejecting the statements of his source; he could not in fact pronounce any scientific verdict on the historicity or otherwise of the alleged march.

Now in the case of the Bible, many of the historical events recorded in it which are of most importance from the religious point of view—and supremely the resurrection—are precisely events in regard to which it is claimed that a pronounced deviation from the normal uniformity of things occurred. That means that though any given historian may, as a Christian, believe that they occurred, he cannot, as an historian, pronounce in their favour, because he has been robbed of the only criterion by which he could judge. In so far, therefore, as we mean by "historical" events, events of which an intelligible account, based upon tested evidence, can be written or given,[1] these vital biblical events can hardly be described as "historical".

[1] Cf. T. A. Roberts, op. cit., pp. 157–8.

I have dealt with this point at some length because it is one, it seems to me, with which theologians will increasingly have to come to terms, in view of what I may call the "Collingwoodian" revolution in historical studies. The modern historian is no longer willing to set the seal of the word "historical" on events, simply because an authority or authorities exist which allege that they happened. The word "historical" is increasingly being reserved for alleged events about which the historian has been able to frame, and answer satisfactorily, certain specific questions. Any historian will admit that there are some alleged past events about which it would be pointless for him to ask his questions because it is in principle impossible for him to answer them. What is more, he will have to admit that, except on certain arbitrary presuppositions, this establishes no presumption against the events in question having occurred; but it does prevent the historian, if he values his integrity, from lending his support to the theologian in describing such events as "historical" in the restricted, but highly important, sense described just now.[1]

To this must be added a further fact. In so far as the character of the biblical narratives does allow of the historian's pronouncing upon them, his verdict, as is well known, has sometimes to be negative; and still more often it has to be the uncertain verdict of "not proven". The combination of this fact with those discussed earlier sets an awkward problem to the

---

[1] In case there should be misunderstanding about the scope of this argument, it may be well to add that of course an individual historian who is a Christian—or even one who is not—may well lend his support to the theologian in believing that some or all of the events described in the Bible did in fact occur; and what is more, he may well believe that he has full rational justification for doing so. The point is, however, that he will be basing this belief on the whole of his experience—including his religious experience—and going beyond the criteria normally employed in "scientific" history. Accordingly, he cannot expect to carry historical colleagues of other metaphysical persuasions with him and so to provide the theologian with independent support for his contentions; in pronouncing on such matters he will himself have become at least half theologian.

If the question is raised whether "scientific" history, so conceived, really exists, that is too big an issue for discussion here; but if it does not, the biblical theologian clearly cannot claim its support for his conclusions.

many modern apologists who lay so much emphasis on the historicity of the events through which the revelation was mediated; and it can lead to statements like the following, which I quote from Professor Alan Richardson's *Introduction to the Theology of the New Testament*, though similar passages can be found in the writings of many other contemporary theologians. Professor Richardson is discussing the Pentecost story in Acts and he writes: "It would therefore seem that a good deal of 'theologizing' lies behind the Lucan Pentecost story; the latter conveys profound Christian truth under the form of a straight-forward historical narrative. But the truth behind the story, namely, that after the exaltation of Christ the pouring out of the Spirit from on high took place, is the plain historical truth, although the Lucan account in Acts 2 is not a literally true story; the literal truth of 'what happened' is not recoverable by us, because the biblical writers, even St Luke, are not chroniclers of the literal. The events as they took place so utterly trans-cended the normal everyday happenings which human language is capable of describing that they could not adequately be recounted in human words at all, and yet they are communi-cable in the wordless language of the Christian experience of the Holy Spirit" (p. 119). I am not sure that I fully understand this passage, but so far as I do, it seems to me to betray a certain embarrassment and also to exhibit such subtlety and sophistication that an outsider might almost be forgiven for suspecting "double-talk". And the same seems to me to be true of a number of the distinctions to be met with in con-temporary theology such as that—again in Professor Richard-son's writings—between "historical truth", or what happened, and "the truth of history" or the spiritual effects of events which are often no longer recoverable by the techniques of the modern historian.

As the quotation from Professor Richardson is enough to show, Christian apologists are fully aware of the work of the historians and its implications and that seems to me to make all the more paradoxical the present situation, in which, at the very moment when the historian is setting question-marks against the historicity of many of the biblical narratives, the apologist seems to be making such historicity the chief plank in his platform. *A propos* of this, Professor C. F. Evans writes in an unpublished paper that he is puzzled by what he describes as "the combination which one comes across fairly frequently, of a dogmatism about the 'historical nature' of Christianity in general and a scepticism about our capacity to recover any of its historical events in particular".

Without retracting anything of what I said earlier about the superiority of a "historical" religion, I do want to question whether, in the extreme form it seems nowadays to have taken, the attempt to establish the historicity of the biblical narratives is any more necessary than it is, in my opinion, likely to succeed. (Incidentally, it is, I think, contrary to the general assumption, something of a novelty in Christian theology.) I should like to suggest that at this point our previous discussion about the mode of revelation, and God's self-limitation in respect of it, has an important application.

Those to whom God addressed himself were not, on the whole, the sort of people—either in virtue of the period when they lived, or in virtue of their personal level of culture—who would naturally have been concerned about precise historical accuracy as we understand it, or indeed able to ensure it if they had been concerned. Have we any reason to think that God overrode their natural trends and capacities in this respect in a way that he did not in other respects? In many cases, the historical events the biblical writers were led to interpret as revelatory, occurred centuries before their time—we may think, for example, of the prophets and the authors of the Pentateuch writing about the exodus. In order to ensure the complete historical accuracy of what they wrote God would have had either to infuse into them a series of ready-made, inerrant, historical propositions, or else to override not only *their* normal capacities and habits of mind but those of all the intervening generations, who would otherwise have created and modified in the process of handing down their historical traditions, as all other people of the period were accustomed to do. Suppose even that some of the events interpreted in the Bible as acts of God are pure (though usually gradual) creations—would that be at all inconsistent with the way we have suggested God went about the work of revelation? Provided we hold on to the essential character of Christianity as in some important sense an historical religion, is there any objection to holding that a part—perhaps even a large part—of God's revelation was through stories which God through his Spirit caused to be told about himself? As we attempt to answer that question let it be kept in mind that some historical incidents in the experience of the biblical writers or their predecessors must have been the occasion for the telling of *these* particular stories about God rather than others. As I have said elsewhere,[1] if we are led to tell fictitious anecdotes about certain outstanding personalities, that is because the people concerned have in hard fact said and done things which make it appropriate to associate those particular anecdotes with them. The *ben trovato* stories told about a given person always have something in common, and if there are enough of them and they derive from different sources, that common element will tell us a good deal about the character and activities of the person of whom they are told.

Perhaps it is another way of making the same point to say, as Professor John Knox rightly does, that we must be very careful in this sort of discussion how precisely we define any biblical event which may be under discussion. If, for example, you define "the event of Christ" as simply the words the earthly Jesus spoke and the actions he performed or the experiences he underwent, the historian's verdict on it will be appreciably different from what it will be if you define the event, as surely you should, so as to include in it the impression the incarnate Christ made on those who had to do with him and the impetus he gave to continuing reflection upon his significance.

There I must leave the historical question, but I realize that

[1] See *The Study of Divinity*, p. 20.

many of you will be asking: "If it is only to a very limited extent that we can turn to the historian for confirmation of what the biblical writers say, to whom are we to turn?" With that vast question I cannot even begin to deal seriously here. Surely the short answer must be that you cannot turn to anyone except yourself, fortified by the experience of the saints who have gone before you. And if that answer were to be developed, would it not have to be along at least two, closely related, lines of argument? The first of these types of argument may be summed up in the words of the Psalmist: "O taste and see how gracious the Lord is." Interpret the universe and live in it as if the biblical writers' accounts of an encounter with a living, loving, demanding, promising God were true, and see if their experience is validated in your own subsequent experience; some such appeal to personal experience is surely unavoidable. But it may be backed up, not only by appeal to the experience of others, but also by the claim that the life lived in accordance with the biblical interpretation of life seems to fit best into the scheme of things and to make sense in the light of conditions as we know them. A few weeks ago a practising psychologist said to me that what most impresses him about Christianity—putting your whole trust in God for life and salvation—is that the state of mind, and attitude to life, to which it gives rise are precisely what he as a psychologist has learned to recognize as true sanity. To become fully convincing the point would need a good deal of qualification and development; but, so qualified and developed, it could be generalized. I hope you see how, for I must now leave the matter there if I am to have time to raise a different question which to me seems both important and puzzling but which, so far as I know, has been comparatively little ventilated, at any rate in this country.

If the account of revelation for which I have been contending is anywhere near the truth, we shall have to conceive the process by which we apprehend the revelation—our reading of the Bible—in terms of overhearing a dialogue or conversation, a dialogue carried on, on the human side, partly in words, but partly in terms of *acted* response. We are all familiar with the intriguing experience of overhearing a snatch of conversation in the street or in a bus or train; sometimes the stretch of dialogue we hear is quite a long one, but even so it cannot in most cases be properly understood without a greater knowledge of the context, and the lives of the people concerned, than we are able to glean from the conversation itself. More than one detective novel I have read has depended on this principle for its *dénouement*, and the same principle applies to the biblical dialogue of revelation. Time and again, the true bearing of a divine communication or a human response only becomes clear in the light of the cultural and historical context, a context which we may have to discover, at some pains, from other parts of the Bible, perhaps from the other Testament, or even from sources outside the Bible altogether. To take an obvious example from the Old Testament, "an eye for an eye and a tooth for a tooth", which may on first hearing sound to modern ears a rather bloodthirsty maxim, turns out, when read in its context, to be a loyal response to a divine demand for greater humanity.

It is a great merit of Father Thornton's in some ways rather strange and perverse book *Revelation and the Modern World* to have emphasized this corollary of the view of revelation we have been discussing. If God has condescended to address men in the full particularity of their peculiar historical and cultural environments, then we have got to immerse ourselves fully and sympathetically in those environments, with their alien customs and values, ways of thinking, and patterns of imagery, before we can understand either his demand or their response. As Father Thornton saw, this lays upon the exegete a tremendous discipline of detailed and far-reaching study, and none has met the demand more diligently, and as a result illuminatingly, than Father Thornton himself—his *Common Life in the Body of Christ* is surely a model for every exegete.

And if anyone who knows that work should ask: "You surely cannot be laying a discipline of that order on every reader of the Bible?" I can only say that I wish I had time to deal with that question fully. Briefly, the assumption that the Bible is a book "who runs may read" is one which has never been shared by the whole of Christendom,[1] and we must allow for the possibility at least that it may turn out to have been to some extent correlative to a particular phase in the understanding of biblical revelation which is now passing away. No one wants a "closed" Bible again, but the doctrine of the "open" Bible, at any rate in the sense defined, is not an article of faith, and it is perhaps a pity that the proposed new Anglican catechism appears to regard the private reading of the Bible as mandatory for every literate member of the Church. Is that realistic, if the study of the Bible involves the sort of thing of which Father Thornton and others have given us a glimpse?[2]

But now for my real difficulty. In the Bible we overhear a dialogue which, as it stands, refers to old and far-off things and battles long ago; how, by overhearing such a dialogue, are we to get light on the quite different moral questions and theological issues of our own day?

It hardly needs emphasizing, in view of what has been said earlier, that this is not a problem with which Christian theologians of an earlier day were troubled in quite the way that we are. Their methods were in some ways like those of the old "scissors-and-paste" historian. Believing, as they did, that what God had revealed in the Bible was a set of propositions, if they wanted biblical guidance about what to believe or how to behave, they set about tracking down such propositions in the Bible as bore directly on the question at issue, convinced that these, if only arranged in a proper synthesis, would yield the necessary guidance as they stood. One is reminded, for example, of the Fathers of Nicaea, who were only with great difficulty

---

[1] Cf. for example the words of John Standish quoted by Professor Rupp on p. 85, and see the discussions on pp. 93f. and 101ff. of Canon Carpenter's essay.

[2] That the attitude reflected in the proposed catechism is by no means new is shown by such passages as those from Archbishop Tenison quoted by Canon Carpenter on p. 116. However, the terms in which Tenison contrasts the Bible and tradition make it clear that his view of the Bible is not one which will easily square with what has been said above.

persuaded to introduce even a single non-biblical term, in the process of drawing out the significance of the biblical revelation for the situation of the year 325. Nor, as we have seen, is such an attitude extinct to-day; we are all familiar with the man who seeks to closure every theological debate by quoting *verbatim* "what the Bible says". Indeed, although such a way of proceeding is incompatible with the modern understanding of biblical revelation, we are all still apt to be hypnotized by it, and, so far as I can see, many theologians are content to assume that once the bearing of the dialogue in its original setting is clear, the process of deriving contemporary illumination from it can be left to take care of itself. How far are they right?

They are obviously right if, with some thinkers, you assume that the sole function of the biblical dialogue is to launch us into a similar dialogue with God, and that then our existential encounter with him will develop its own momentum, as it were, and lead on to a continuing relationship, which will itself dictate, from time to time, what further approach to the Bible may be necessary and how it should be made. According to Bultmann, the revelation of Jesus is just this, that he *is* the Revealer.

There is clearly important truth here; and on any view we must be careful to do full justice in this connection to the work of the Holy Spirit. At least since the time of writing of John 16 it has been recognized as one of the Spirit's functions to make the biblical revelation contemporary to each generation of Christians by his internal testimony within them. But the whole economy of revelation, as we have understood it, suggests that the Holy Spirit will do his work by co-operation with our intellectual and cognitive capacities, and not by superseding them; we must surely beware of what I may call the "magical occasionalism" to which Dr Karl Barth seems sometimes in danger of succumbing—I mean the idea that the Holy Spirit will make Bible reading an occasion for infusing into our minds truths not in any way integrally related to the contents of the particular passage under consideration. While we dare not set any limits to the modes of the Spirit's working, it will be obvious that if this account of his working were carried to an extreme, we should have to say that he could equally well use the reading of any other book—or indeed the performance of any other activity—as the occasion of his infusions of truth, and the Bible would be robbed of any peculiar function in the mediation of revelation.

So, however exactly the Holy Spirit helps us to understand the biblical revelation, we must surely assume that the process will be analogous at least to that by which we apprehend the meaning of any other book; and accordingly questions about the best method of approach and proper principles of interpretation cannot be avoided. How do we derive a modern Christianity from the overhearing of an ancient dialogue?

Our only clue now to God's part in the biblical dialogue is the recorded words and actions of the human participants. In following up that clue, two things need constantly to be kept in mind.

First, that the human exposition of the revelation is always compounded not only of the revelation itself but also of ideas and presuppositions already in the recipient's mind quite apart from his acceptance of the revelation he is seeking to expound.[1] These ideas and presuppositions were sometimes such that when they came together with the revelation the result was mutual illumination; but also, surely, *pace* Father Thornton, they were sometimes of such a character as to obscure or distort the divine demand.

The second point is really an extension of the first. We have seen that it was himself that God was seeking to reveal, and God is greater than the measure of men's minds in any age; consequently what the original recipients of the revelation could comprehend and put into words could never be more than a part of the full truth being revealed; and so, as Professor Hodgson expresses it, "The real object of our study is not what

[1] See L. Hodgson, *For Faith & Freedom*, i. p. 112.

the men whose works we are reading were *consciously aware* of thinking and saying; it is the truth which was struggling to make itself known through minds conditioned by their pre-suppositions"—and, we may add, darkened by their sins.[1] At first sight these two considerations might seem to place the modern interpreter in an impossible situation. For it might appear that in order to have any basis for judging how far the unsuitable thought-forms and the inevitable human limitation of the original recipients distorted or obscured the revelation, he would need independent access to the revelation, which *ex hypothesi* he cannot have. Father Thornton was quite right to draw our serious attention to this problem, though perhaps he allowed himself to be too much daunted by it. But before we consider that, it may be useful to draw a distinction.

What we want from the Bible is guidance both of a moral and also of a more strictly doctrinal, or metaphysical, kind. If it is permissible for practical purposes to make such a rough and ready distinction, and to deal first with the moral aspect of the matter, may we not say that, just as, through continual conversation with a person, you "get to know his mind", and become able to judge what he would want or approve in a given situation, so, through fully immersing ourselves in the biblical dialogue, sympathetically studied with the aid of all scholarly insights, we may come to know the mind of God and learn to judge his will and demand in the situations with which we are confronted.

There is, I know, one obvious objection to saying this, namely that biblical interpreters to all appearances equally steeped in the biblical dialogue, often disagree about God's mind on such contemporary questions, for example, as nuclear armaments or the economic ordering of modern industrial society. This fact is unquestionably an important one, but I do not think it tells against my argument; quite apart from the fact that some are better qualified to interpret the Scriptures than others, the conclusion to be drawn is surely that the Bible is not meant to

[1] Op. cit., p. 114, italics mine.

be a quarry from which answers to the moral and social questions of each age can be dug out ready made. What is true, I suggest, is that those who come to the solution of contemporary problems from a deep and sympathetic acquaintance with the biblical dialogue will be found to approach them with the same basic attitude (someone has actually coined the phrase "agapaistic personalism"!) and that within that biblically-conditioned attitude it is left to us to work out our own solutions to contemporary problems, of course not without the Spirit's help. Sometimes some particular biblical parallel will spring to mind in connection with a modern problem, for after all we share the basic humanity of the biblical men and women and such parallels can be very enlightening; but if we are wise, we shall, I think, always be cautious about absolutizing any particular biblical injunction or precedent, remembering the deep gulf between its context and our situation. "The Bible says . . ." can never be a final arbiter.

However, it is when we come to the doctrinal or metaphysical aspect of the matter that the questions seem to me to be extremely perplexing and at the same time strangely little discussed. You will all remember Professor Hodgson's by now almost hackneyed formulation of the problem: "If the truth about God's revelation . . . be such that those men saw it and wrote of it like that, what must it be for us?"[1] Well yes—but what *must* it be? How are we to tell? Perhaps for the sake of brevity and vividness, I may put the question in personal categories. St Paul, in the light of his share in the dialogue, and his knowledge of the earlier dialogue, made certain statements about what God had done in Christ; but if he were here now, how would he put it? Or, to sharpen the question, how would he himself know how to put it? In the first century, for example, he spoke of the atonement in terms of the conquest of supernatural forces of evil. How would he know, if he were here to-day, whether the present tendency on the part of some highly-placed Anglicans to discount the devil and his subordinates is a passing phase of

[1] Op. cit., p. 88.

mid-twentieth-century thought, which needs correcting in the light of the biblical understanding, or whether it is justified and so evidence that in this respect Paul's own first-century thought was conditioned by contemporary culture rather than by the revelation itself? And if sacrificial rather than demonological categories were to be taken as the example, the question would no doubt receive an even sharper point.

Well, first, I think, we have to face the fact that even St Paul could not know, in one quite legitimate sense of the word. Even on the basis of the Bible it is not given us to know the will of God; "that", as Father Kelly once said, "is the giddy joke". What we have to do is to stop looking for knowledge in this sense, for the sort of absolute answers that are not given, and try to discover a way of approaching the Bible that is likely to discover its message for our day with the least likelihood of distortion.

The general clue lies, once again, in Father Thornton's book, where he insists that God's activity in revelation and incarnation is always parallel to his creative and providential activity. This is surely right, though Father Thornton himself seems not to have drawn out its full implications for our discussion. It surely means that without taking up an infallibilist position towards the modern world-view or the pronouncements of the contemporary scientist—for modern thinkers and scientists have been at least as opaque to the revelation of truth as the men and women of the Bible—we have got to recognize that the various inventions and discoveries which have brought us so far from the biblical world are themselves God-given, and so are, in their measure, a medium of divine self-disclosure. If so, the full revelation will come through the fruitful interplay between the insights God has granted to the modern world and the revelation vouchsafed to the men of the Bible. Just as the insights of the Bible must be allowed to judge the arrogance and arbitrariness of many modern presuppositions, so the truth in modern insights can help us to refine and modify the biblical statements as they stand, so that they may more directly disclose their revelatory content to us.

Here, more than anywhere else in theology, we are the victims of specialization. Most biblical scholars are admirably equipped by linguistic and historical studies to interpret the various books of the Bible in the light of their original context; but when it comes to the sort of confrontation between the biblical writers' outlook and the modern outlook, of which I have spoken, most biblical scholars are at best amateurs. They consider the problem, if at all, only piecemeal, and, as a result, its full implications and seriousness often remain obscured from them. It is to the credit of one biblical scholar, Professor Rudolf Bultmann, that he has attempted to cope with this problem in a comprehensive way, attempting to discover what are the essential characteristics of the modern outlook from this point of view and so seeking to find what he calls a hermeneutic principle with which to interpret the biblical revelation as a whole. The illuminating insights with which his *New Testament Theology* abounds are largely true to this pioneering attempt on his part, but the trouble with his attempt is that it is too summary and too arbitrary. He explicitly absolutizes the existential theories of Martin Heidegger as the final philosophical analysis of the modern situation, and when he summarizes its significance for biblical exegesis at the beginning of *Kerygma and Myth*, his very brief statement contains many arbitrary assumptions, and lumps together such very different issues as the astronomy, the demonology, and the eschatology of first-century man. What I plead is that we should have some biblical scholars who come to their study from a background of professional philosophy and other "modern" studies, and whose expertise is, if I may put it so, in the modern end of the problem. Perhaps in the light of their studies they might even do for us what Bultmann has tried to do, more systematically, and at the same time more tentatively and empirically. What they might produce need make no claim to be a full or final analysis of the modern *Weltanschauung* or even of its religious implications; but would not some such analysis be of inestimable value to all serious students of the Bible, as helping to clarify their thinking about the size and character of the ultimate problem they are up against?

Can the modern reader make sense of "sacrifice", "expiation", "recapitulation", "mystical incorporation", and such concepts, or do the passages of the dialogue in which they occur need some degree of "demythologization"? If so, how much and in what terms? No one expects that such questions will be quickly or finally answered, but surely systematic study of them would help; I suggest that they deserve much more explicit and concentrated study in relation to the biblical problem than is, so far as I know, being given to them.

Selective Index of Names and Subjects